Believe

You

Can

Clive Gott

Believe You Can

Believe You Can is written and published by Clive Gott

For details of this and other publications by Clive Gott contact:

Clive Gott
15 Toll Bar Way
Tadcaster
North Yorkshire
LS24 8JT

www.clivegott.com

Email: clive@clivegott.com

This book is dedicated to

Sara
My sweetheart my lover and my friend

Laura
My continued education and enlightenment

And to all of those people who have chosen to live their lives by design and not by default, who have chosen to challenge their limiting beliefs, and who have decided that whatever it is they choose to attempt, the greatest quality of all is to

Believe They Can.

"You are not what you think you are
What you think, you are."
Anon

"We become what we think
about most of the time."
Earl Nightingale

"Success is not the result of spontaneous
combustion. First you have to set your
self on fire."
Anon

Introduction

I have been meaning to write this book for ages, years even. But for some reason I have been putting it off over and over again. I have some really good reasons for delaying writing it, however we all know the real reason don't we? In truth I was scared. Why would someone who left school in 1974 with nothing but a negative report card and an ability to mimic the pop artists of the day think that they could string together enough words to hold an intelligent conversation, let alone write a full book? In fact until the late 1980s I had never even read another book since leaving school. So what is this all about then? Well I guess I am writing it for a lot of reasons. There is the value it may well bring to some people's lives when they have read it. There is the challenge of doing something people like me "just don't do." There is the inevitable achievement of completing it. And who knows, perhaps one day we will see it on the list of the top twenty best sellers in Borders? It might even make me a few quid. But the real reason I'm writing it is because I want to, and I believe I can. And if I can then so can you, if you "Believe You Can."

My method of writing is fairly simple, I write as I speak. It is my intention that when you read this book it will read as though I am speaking only to you. With that in mind I would like you to write your name in the blank space provided at the beginning of the book. That way it will be your book, and all of the thoughts and ideas that you have as a result of reading it will be your own private thoughts and ideas.

Although this book is for sale there are certain people who will receive a copy from the first print run as a gift from me. The first of these people, and in fact the very first book, will go to my Mum. Finally she will be able to understand what it is that I do all day and where some of those crazy ideas I have come from. The second copy will of course go to my beautiful wife Sara. If nothing else it will prove that I have been doing something constructive when I have got out of bed at six o'clock in the morning. And it might give

Believe You Can

some hint of reason as to why I wake up in the middle of the night to go to the office and write down a great idea for the opening line of the next chapter before I forget it. I will give a copy to my daughter Laura. She goes to University this year and a good book will stop the table wobbling. The truth is that, whether she reads it or not, she will keep it where her friends can see it because despite what I might sometimes think she is enormously proud of her Dad.

I intend to give a copy each to two very rare animals (in my life anyway). They are Chris Keys and Stephanie White. These two are the two teachers who I remember with most affection from my school days. There are plenty that I remember for the wrong reasons. Like the one who wrote: "Gott needs to understand that he will achieve nothing by talking all day!" Stephanie taught me from when I was a twelve year old to when I left school. She allowed me to rebel against woodwork and metalwork to do needlework and cookery. Not only can I now sew on a button myself but I can also cook a five-course meal as well as most people I know. And I can *still* make a mean Victoria sponge. Stephanie also affords me the privilege of working with her students on a regular basis as a part of their education. Chris taught me to play rugby and knew how to laugh during a lesson. He is well over fifty now but he still looks like a thirty year old. Chris is one of those guys who you just know you would admire no matter what he did. But fortunately for the students of Tadcaster Grammar School he chose education as his vocation.

The other copy will go to my great friend Russ. Russ was the supportive and advisory half of the two-person conversation that started "I'm thinking of going it alone and starting my own business. What do you think?" His advice and questions helped me to make one of the most courageous and rewarding decisions I have ever made. I also have many friends who I will give a copy to. They are too numerous to mention here but they know who they are. A heart felt thank you to you all for your continued support and inspiration.

Believe You Can

I have written this book from my heart. In it there are lots of stories about, and references to, people and events that you may well have read or heard about before. There is nothing new in "Believe You Can," just the same old stuff presented in my own inimitable style. The same old stuff that is so often referred to as common sense. The truth is though that so few people use it that it should really be referred to as uncommon sense. If you have read some of the stuff in other books, or heard other speakers using the same references, neither they nor I have stolen them from each other. We have just borrowed them off the next person to come along and use them. So enjoy the read and when you have finished please feel free to contact me and let me know what it is that you now *"Believe You Can."*

On the next page there is a space to write your name so that you can personalise the messages in this book. There is also a space for you to write out a burning question. My guess is that this is probably not the first personal development book you have read. If that is the case you, like many others, and me, are probably looking for some answers. One of the most frustrating things I have found about searching for answers is that I sometimes don't even know what the question is. Now is your chance to find out.

Before you read this book any further ask yourself what the one question is that you would like answering about yourself and your personal development or future achievements, if you knew the answer was in here? Just ask the question and then write it down. Then go one step further and write down what it would mean to you if you found the answer. At the end there will be space for you to re-write the question along with the answer, if indeed you found it in the pages of my book. It will be my pleasure to receive the questions you were looking for along with the answer that you found. If you didn't find the answer please send the question anyway and I will do my very best to help you find the answer you are looking for.

I wish you happy reading and learning.

A burning question

When Clive wrote this book he was speaking to me. My name is:

_____

The burning question I would like to find an answer to in the pages of this book is:

_____

_____

_____

Finding the answer to my question will allow me to:

_____

_____

_____

Spotted on an Adidas shop window

Impossible is just a big word thrown around by small men who find it easier to live in a world they've been given than to explore the power they have to change it. Impossible is not a fact it is an opinion. Impossible is not a declaration it is a dare. Impossible is potential. Impossible is temporary.

Impossible is nothing.

Forever sport adidas.

A couple of definitions

Throughout this book you will see me referring (affectionately) to *'Tree Huggers'* and *'Outboard Motors.'* The definitions are:

Tree Huggers: People who constantly live their lives at fifteen on a scale of one-to-ten. Their glass is not just half full it is positively overflowing. If their backside were on fire they would put it out with petrol and smile when they were doing it. *Nothing* is negative therefore there is no need for this stuff.

Outboard Motors: These people are complete opposites to the aforementioned *Tree Huggers.* Outboard motors walk around all day saying "but", "but" "but" "but" (say but, but over and over again very fast if you don't get the joke!). For every good idea you have they will find three reasons why it won't work. "But we tried that!" "But what if it doesn't work?" Yada yada yada! Avoid these people like the plague. In fact, if you want to see something quite spectacular, why not introduce them to a tree hugger and watch them both implode?

A few others you should avoid:

Bloke says: This is the guy in the pub who knows everything about nothing. A particularly dangerous Outboard this one because they are very adept at convincing you to think again because they are "sure it won't work" or even worse still they "know someone who tried it, can't remember their name right now, but they ended up in all sorts of trouble." These people should be identified and avoided at all costs. They can serve no real or positive purpose in your future success.

They: Usually mentioned on news items as being responsible for new research invariably telling us not to do something we have been enjoying for many years. 'They' have done some research. Or 'they' have discovered whatever will kill you if you keep using it. A simple question for you to ask 'them' when they go off on one and start telling you to change your life is, "How do you know?"

Why YOU should read this book.

Outboard Motor's thoughts:
"You probably shouldn't! All of these books are the same," (outboard motors are prone to generalisation), "full of fancy ideas and clever thinking that only works if you have money."

Author's thoughts:
Everyone, yes EVERYONE, has the power to dream. We all have the power to close our eyes and visualise how we wish things could be or how we hope things will be. There are absolutely no limits to the things we can dream of or the things we wish we could do, have, be, create or become. If you were to close your eyes now you could visualise yourself in the perfect relationship, with the perfect partner. Within seconds you could be walking down a secluded beach or flying a supersonic aircraft. You could be playing with your own children or finishing a marathon in under four hours. We can even close our eyes and visualise ourselves looking fit and healthy and having a physical presence to die for.

And we don't always have to make it so distant. If we choose to we can make it a lot simpler and closer to home. **Imagine having the perfect day at work. How about imagining a weekend or a evening when you do exactly what you want, where you want, with whom you want, and for as long as you want.** You can do that. I can do that (I very often do), in fact we can all do that. All we have to do is close our eyes and make some pictures. With visualisation and dreams we can literally be anyone, anywhere with anything.

The challenge for most people though is that when they open their eyes the dream ends. It's "back to the real world." A world where, like it or not, we take what we are given. Where arguments and divorce are an accepted part of life. Where "kids will be kids." Where "no matter what I eat I can't lose weight." Where money goes to money and the only way most of us can be as "lucky" as Richard Branson is to win the lottery. In fact for a great many people the dream thing starts with the question in the pub or over dinner: "What would you do if you won the lottery?"

It is perhaps time for us to realise that the lottery win is not coming. Neither is the rich uncle, the perfect job, your ideal partner, your dream holiday or the fastest car on earth, or anything else you "wish" you could have for that matter. None of these things are coming. ***But all of them*** (*perhaps with the exception of the rich uncle and the lottery*) *are waiting for you to go out there and get them.*

I truly believe that there has never been a better time for us to achieve our dreams and goals. Despite all of what we read or see in the media the world has been set up for us all to succeed, in whatever field we choose. Especially in the UK. Oh sure, if you ask them, the outboards will spend all day telling you about the way life is set up for the rich to get richer and the happy to get happier. But these people only achieve their success because they have taken a chance and survived. It is an absolute fact that in the UK today you can wake up one morning with a fantastic idea for a new business buzzing around in your head. You can think of a name for your new venture (check with companies house that someone else is not already using it), find yourself a printer who will knock you up some business cards and letter heads, and you are off. If done by the book you have done nothing illegal so far. You are now left with a choice, to work very hard and make it work or to do very little and watch it fail. And these are just some of the choices we are able to make today. There has never been a greater demand for knowledge than now.

Starting up in whatever you want to do was never put more powerfully than when the American speaker Larry Wingett told us to "find your uniqueness and then find a way to exploit that uniqueness." All you need is a dream.

This book has been written to help you realise that you *can* live the dream. You *can* reach another level in your life, in your relationships, financially, physically, even in your career. You can achieve whatever it is that you want, but you must first know what it is that you want to achieve. Now here is the really good news. To start you on the journey to achieving at least some of the things you believe will make you happy and fulfilled you do not need to go back to college or sit a masters degree (unless of course one of the things you want is to go back to college or sit a masters degree). **You already have everything you will ever need within you right now to start the journey to the life you truly desire for yourself.**

You are already an excellent achiever, or you wouldn't be reading this book right now. Now is the time for you to move forward and become an outstanding achiever. The gap between the two levels is not wide and does not require years of gathering knowledge (though you may find yourself wanting to find out more) or acquiring new skills. You have everything inside you right now to become more than you already are. I challenge you to release your potential and to realise your dreams. I understand that right now you might be thinking, "If only I could, but I can't." The truth is you might be right, maybe you can't. ***But what if you could?***

If you want to achieve something you have never achieved you have to become someone you have never been.

Why are some people more successful than others?

So what is the difference between success and mediocrity?

Outboard Motor's answer:

"MONEY! Money goes to money! You are either born lucky (?) like that Branson bloke or born to work for people like that Branson bloke. I'm just off to buy my lottery ticket now. I don't know why I bother though. I will never win. People like me never do!"

Author's answer:

Wow! What a question. The truth is that people have been asking this question since the days of Babylon. Why do some people seem to have it all whilst others appear to have to struggle through life accepting whatever crumbs are swept off the great table of life after everyone else has finished? Why, if we are all supposed to start with a clean sheet in life, are there some people who seem to have the perfect relationship, or wonderfully well behaved kids? Why are those people able to take more than one holiday a year when others struggle to take just one. How come of the two people in an organisation who both have the same qualifications and have both been exposed to the same levels of training, one of them is flying high looking at promotion, whilst the other is hanging on to their job by the skin of their teeth?

The reason, therefore the answer to this question, is simple. Successful people *think* differently. And that's the bottom line! We have to think. It is a basic requirement for life. Everything we do starts off as a simple thought. So if we have to think, doesn't it make more sense to think empowering thoughts?

Instead of "I can't" why not ask "What if I could?" In his recording "The Strangest Secret", Earl Nightingale tells us "We become what we think about." Therefore, if we constantly think about how we can make something happen it will eventually become so. Likewise, if you constantly think about reasons why something won't or can't happen it too will become so. If you constantly ask "Why me?" the universe will oblige you by showing you why you! If, on the other hand, you always ask "Why not me?" or "What if I could?" the same universe will be obliged to provide the solution you seek.

Think about it this way. Have you ever had an experience in your life (perhaps you are going through it right now) where all you want to do is pay off your debts? Every time you get somewhere close to paying off those debts something happens where you have to spend a sum of money that immediately puts you back where you were. The reason is that you are always thinking of yourself as being in debt. You see if your goal is always to pay off your debts, the one thing you must have to achieve your goal is debt. What if you set a goal to be debt free and have a sum of money in the bank, untouched? How would you be thinking about yourself then? You would think of yourself as someone who is saving money to invest in your future. I know what you might be thinking, "aren't they the same goal?" And the answer is yes they are. Or at least the outcome is the same. But the way you *think* about yourself is different. The same applies when you are trying to lose weight. If your goal is to lose weight then you have to think of yourself as overweight to have that goal. However, if you think of yourself as someone who is becoming lighter, fitter and healthier so that you can achieve … whatever, you will start to think of yourself as a healthy person as opposed to a fat or overweight person.

Have you ever noticed how angry or frustrated you become when your thoughts are constantly related to your problems, and how much bigger your problem becomes the more you think about it? Well it works just as well the other way around. If you are constantly looking for a solution and using statements like I can" or "How can I?" or "What if I could?" you will be directed towards finding positive answers and outcomes.

Knowledge and skill are always good to have around in times of challenge. But sometimes knowledge and skill are a little like having a credit card with a £10,000 balance when the shop only takes cash. It looks good, it makes you feel fantastic to have it, but when you need to have something else it is totally useless. No I'm not decrying knowledge and skill here, I have some myself that I use on a regular basis.

I am also constantly working to increase my quota of both. What I am saying is that they are of little or no use on their own. The world is full of educated failures. There are also many stories and examples of 'ignorant' or undereducated successes. Take me for example. I left school with nothing (except a report card that said, "generally a nuisance who will probably amount to nothing," hmmm) and now I'm writing a book and travelling the world as a professional speaker. (I am actually writing this part of my book in the beautiful Emirate of Dubai.) No, I'm not saying that knowledge and skill are of no use to their owner, they are. But they will be of infinitely more use if they are used in conjunction with high self-esteem and unshakeable self-belief. Knowing the rules of a game does not make you an International athlete. Likewise, knowing everything about your product and attending every sales course you can find will not bring you the salesperson of the year award. Simply knowing what and how will never be enough to help you to realise your dreams and ambitions.

In the pages of this book we are going to explore some of the areas that I believe will give us that added extra when it comes to becoming successful. For the record we will define success as "moving towards whatever is important to you in your life." In the main we will explore certain areas that I believe we must pay attention to in order to bridge the gap between mediocrity and success.

The areas we will cover are:

- **Developing and maintaining high self-esteem**
- **Developing and maintaining a positive attitude**
- **Developing unshakeable self-confidence**
- **Developing an empowering belief system**
- **Learning how to sustain personal motivation**
- **Learning how to set and achieve personal and professional goals**

Please be aware though that in the pages of this book I can only introduce you to these elements of success. Like all other elements of personal development and success they must be learned and practiced, constantly. "What if You Could?" has no pass or fail, you will not get a certificate of completion when you have finished the book. You will only know that you have perhaps challenged some of your limiting beliefs and in doing so set yourself on a journey of success and achievement that you previously thought impossible. **So make your next shot your best and adopt a better question as your guide for your future.**

"I know I can't, but **What If I Believed I Could?"**

If all you had to do to make something happen was to believe it was possible what would you believe it was possible for you to achieve?

Developing and maintaining high self-esteem

The most important person in your life.

Outboard motor's thoughts:

"It's every man for himself in this world. We came with nowt (nothing if you are North of London) and we will leave with nowt so we have to take what we can while we are here."

Author's thoughts:

If you have ever flown on an aeroplane and actually listened to the flight instructions you will have heard the attendants tell you that, "in the unlikely event of a reduction in cabin pressure oxygen masks will drop from the overhead locker. *Put your own on first before you put on anyone else's.*" (Strewth, I guess I must have listened.) The airlines realised long ago that you are the most important person in your life. I know that right about now some of you want to tell me about your beautiful children and your adoring partner who you love with your whole being. I know you do because I used to think the same. But what the airlines have recognised is, that if you do not look after yourself, you will not be able to look after your loved ones. It's not selfish, just common sense to look after yourself.

So what would this mean to our lives, you know, in the unlikely event that we would decide that we were indeed the most important person in our lives? How many times have you been somewhere you don't really want to go or done something you don't really want to do, just because you felt you should? "What would people think if I didn't show?" Well here is something to think about. (Perhaps you should read the next statement and then put the book down for a while, just to think about what I am about to say.)

What other people think of you is none of your business!

Wouldn't it be wonderful if that statement was true? If we could write it on our mirrors and walls and carry it in our wallets and purses knowing that all we had to do was to look at it often enough and it would become the truth. "If only!" But what if it was true.

Believe You Can

What if other people's opinions of us were none of our business? What would you do with your time, and ultimately your life, that you dare not do now for fear of upsetting or offending someone?

In truth we do sometimes need the approval of others. Your boss at work for example for an idea you would like to try out. Your spouse or partner for an investment you would like to make, or even your children for the choice of holiday you are thinking of taking. This is not the same as constantly seeking the approval of others for the decisions YOU make with YOUR life. You should not have to constantly justify the choices you take with regards to the people you choose as friends or life partners, or the clothes you choose to wear, or even the car you drive, or the social life you choose to lead. These are your choices and as such are not any business of other people. Oh I'm certain other people will want to pass an opinion on the things we have mentioned. But their opinion will be based upon the choices that they would have taken given the same circumstances. What that means is that other people's opinions of you are none of your business because they are based purely on their opinions of how they would run their own business. Acceptance of these facts is, I believe, the foundation of developing high self-esteem.

Developing high self-esteem.

Outboard motor's thoughts:
"Self, self, self that's you lot all over isn't it?"

Author's thoughts:
I have said it before and will keep repeating it because I believe it to be fact. High self-esteem is a basic requirement for success. It is our level of self-esteem that allows us to appreciate other people for who, or what, they are. Typically, high self-esteem people will like and value, themselves and others. They will have confidence in their own opinions whilst still valuing yours. It might help in our quest to develop high self-esteem if we first understood a little more of what

self-esteem is. Well the Collins English dictionary gives the following definition of what the word esteem means:

Esteem: To have respect or high regard for

Ipso facto Self-Esteem must mean:

To have respect or high regard for yourself

Put simply, your self-esteem is your own opinion of you. From the day we are born our self-esteem is under construction. Obviously we cannot affect our own self-esteem at such an early age so we are at the mercy of those around us. The first influence on the way we perceive ourselves is usually our parents, or at least whoever is responsible for our initial thoughts and beliefs about ourselves and our abilities.

As time goes on other influences, such as our environment and our teachers, will have an effect on how we perceive ourselves, and later in life it will be our work environment and the people we choose to associate with. If we are constantly told we are hard working, polite and intelligent then the chances are that we will grow towards those attributes and develop a self-concept that reflects them. If on the other hand we are constantly referred to as lazy or ignorant it is just as likely that we will lean towards those attributes instead. I cringe when I am introduced to a child and told, in front of the child, that he or she is shy. The actions of the child, both at the time and probably later in life, usually reflect the image being portrayed by the person in question and then we are surprised when the child grows into a quiet and retiring adult. Hmmm!

"SO!" I hear you cry, "Can we determine the level of our own self-esteem as we grow older and wiser?" And my answer is a resounding, "YES, please do." And now I guess you want me to tell you how don't you?

Well, by the end of this book, I expect you to have a much higher opinion of yourself than you do now. Everything I am going to write about is designed, in some way or other, to help you to develop your self-concept. But I will give you a few tips just to keep you going for a while until we get to the juicy bits like empowering beliefs and goal setting. Here are a few things you can try right now to start growing your self-esteem.

Accept yourself for who you are.

It is an undeniable fact that you are who you are right now, so accept that. The chances are that you bought this book because there are one, or a few, aspects of yourself that you would like to change. Well congratulations to you for making the decision to take responsibility for your future. Before we can pay off our debts or lose some weight we first have to know exactly how much we owe or how much we weigh. Once we have figured that out we have to accept the situation as it is and then make a decision to change. Well the same applies to you. Once you have figured out who you are, and perhaps what you would like to change about yourself, you can accept yourself for who you are and decide to take action to change whatever it is you have decided to change.

Say this to yourself out loud, as often as you feel is necessary to let it sink in:

"I am who I am right now and I accept that."

Now follow the previous statement with this one:

"Who I am and what I am today is the worst I will ever be."

That second statement is particularly exciting because even if you perceive yourself as already being successful, you will be even more so tomorrow. WOW what a concept.

23

Approve of yourself.

Whether you realise it or not everything you have done in your life to this point has been for the best intentions. You have done the very best you could with the knowledge you had available at the time. I think that is worthy of approval don't you? Oh I'm certain that if I asked you to you could list, with absolute clarity, the things that you have done wrong. Those things that, if you had your time over, you would never consider doing again. I think if we are honest we all could. But how many things have you swept under the carpet that you could, if you chose to, be very proud of? My guess is that there will be as many, if not more, of the latter than the former. Well done you. Now say well done to yourself and let's move on. Say it.... Go on, say it..."Well done me." (There that didn't hurt too much did it?)

Appreciate yourself.

Have you ever muttered those immortal words "If only people would appreciate me more?" Or "No one ever says well done to me for my efforts." Well how do you expect people to appreciate you if you never appreciate yourself?

What have you done lately that you could say "well done me" for?
What are you good at?
What have you ever done magnificently?
What do you really appreciate about yourself?
What is fantastic about your attitude?
What would your work colleagues say if they were only allowed to speak positively about you for ten minutes each?
What have you done to make sure that the world is a better place for you having been in it?

Answering these questions (more than once) will remind you of your good points. Next time you find yourself being less than complimentary to yourself stop yourself straight away and think of something you appreciate about you. It will help you to stay focused on the magnificent you and away from the person that you think needs to change.

Give yourself permission to be less than perfect.

We ALL make mistakes. In reality it is the mistakes we make that aid our learning. Next time you do something that you would normally chastise or ridicule yourself for why not just say to yourself (out loud again if you like) "that's OK, I never claimed to be perfect and I am allowed to make mistakes and learn from them."

Speak to yourself with respect.

How often do you say something to yourself that would offend you if someone else said it to you? Why do we do this? My guess is because most people who use negative self-talk don't appreciate the damage it does to us. They think that because they are saying it to themselves, and that no one else can hear what they say, there will be no damage done. Not the case I'm afraid. Just because it is you who is saying it doesn't make it any less damaging. Your poor unconscious mind doesn't know the difference between your voice and another voice. It will follow instructions no matter who gives them.

One of the most positive gifts you can give yourself is to learn the art of positive self-talk. You are the only person who will be with you until the end, every second of every day. With that in mind I guess it makes sense to get on with yourself doesn't it?

When you do something right, or well, give yourself a verbal reward. Say "Well done me." on a daily basis every time you are successful at anything. Ask yourself better questions than you might normally do. When you find yourself in a situation that would normally prompt a "Why me?" question, ask instead "What can I do to get out of this situation?" If you catch yourself calling yourself a "stupid idiot" (or even worse if you play golf) say something like "That's not like me, how can I do it differently?" Let's stick with that golf thing.

25

Believe You Can

(If you don't play golf relate this to your life in some other way.) Imagine you have just hit a drive two hundred metres down the fairway and your ball has landed smack bang in the middle of a bunker. Instead of the usual abuse and expletives why not say something like "Wow what a shot. To hit a ball that far and have it land in a patch of sand so small in comparison to the size of the fairway is something special. And how fortunate I am that I recently bought a new sand iron. This will be an ideal opportunity to test it out. This surely is a wonderful learning experience." Now don't you think that would make you feel much better than "*;!*$+@>:**?#~"<# useless clubs?" (Disclaimer here. You will probably end up finishing the game on your own.)

In short, I suggest you learn to talk yourself up instead of putting yourself down. After all, who else is going to hear you?

Just as a starter to ease you gently into positive self-talk, you could start by eliminating certain words and phrases from your vocabulary altogether. For the next twenty-four hours catch yourself, and then stop yourself from using some of the following phrases:

I have to
I need to
I must
I can't
I might

And finally, the ultimate in negative, "hold me back I'm procrastinating" self-talk answer to the question, "When will you (I) start?"

"I might, perhaps, probably, if everything goes right, assuming there are no hold ups, if I'm moving down hill with a tail wind, if I am really lucky, assuming I can find the time, I would like to think I could get started by Friday, ish!"

How many reasons are there in just that one sentence for not getting started at whatever your goal is. A better, more positive, answer to the same question would simply be "Friday."

Find yourself a coach or a mentor.

A mentor could be described as "an advisor" whilst a coach could be described as "a vehicle for longer journeys." Both, or either, are important in helping you to raise and maintain positive self-esteem. A mentor will be someone who has already achieved the level that you aspire to be at. They might even have achieved whatever it is that you are working towards.

Your mentor can advise you and help you to avoid some of the pitfalls that you might face along your journey. They will probably have experience in the field in which you are aspiring to be successful. Your mentor, like all successful people, will be willing to pass on that help and advice. Their reward will be to watch your growth.

Your coach however, could, and in some cases should, be someone who has NOT achieved in your chosen field. They will be someone you can use as a sounding board. Your coach will not pass an opinion on your ideas; remember they might not have any experience in your chosen field. They will be there to listen and to ask those questions that you either dare not ask yourself or that you have forgotten to ask yourself.

If you are not who you want to be right now
pretend that you are until you get there.

So now that we understand a little more about our self-esteem and how to develop it, let's move on to probably the most important ingredient in developing positive self-esteem, and that is developing and maintaining a positive attitude.

Developing and maintaining a positive attitude

Developing a positive attitude.

Outboard motor's thoughts:

"I don't believe in having a positive attitude. If you expect the worst to happen there is less chance of you being disappointed isn't there? The only thing I am positive about is that things will go wrong. I'm positive they will."

Author's thoughts:

I have been called all sorts over the last ten years or so. An evangelist, unrealistic (whatever that means) and yes even a tree hugger, along with a few other things it would not be polite to print in the pages of this book. The one thing I have not been called too often is a bloke with a positive attitude to life. But in truth that is all I am. I have made certain choices about how I react to certain things and it is those choices that bring about my attitude.

Choice. A simple word yet one that many people don't believe in. Yet it is a word that is relevant to all of us. It is worth remembering that it is not what happens to us in life that gives us a positive or negative outlook. It is how we **choose** to react to what happens to us in life that gives us a positive or negative outlook.

Have you ever been waiting for an aeroplane or a train that has been delayed? If you have did you look around and observe the reactions of the other people in the same situation as yourself? Why is it that some people accept that the plane, or train, is late and choose to read or relax while others choose to walk up and down demanding to know when the situation will be resolved and complaining that "this is the worst airline or train operating company they have ever seen?"

The same can apply in traffic jams. Some of us, me included, accept that there is nowhere to go and accept that as fact, whilst others get out of their cars (or stay in their cars for that matter) and very slowly start to microwave themselves from the inside eventually glowing like a beacon. Don't these people realise that however they choose to react the traffic really doesn't care about them. The absolute truth is that in all of these situations, and other similar situations for that matter, the people in question have made a choice. They have chosen to **respond** positively to a situation that they can do nothing about. Or they have chosen to **react** negatively to the same situation that they too can do nothing about.

Breaking the habit.

Our attitudes are habits, and like any habit we can change them. Firstly, it might help if we look at how our attitudes are formed.

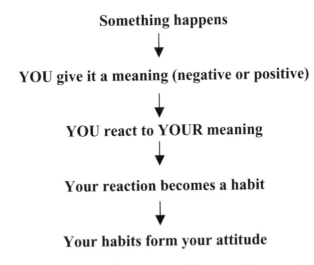

Something happens

↓

YOU give it a meaning (negative or positive)

↓

YOU react to YOUR meaning

↓

Your reaction becomes a habit

↓

Your habits form your attitude

A simple yet wonderfully descriptive diagram of how we form our attitudes don't you think? Let's explore the diagram.

Something happens.

Every minute of every day something is happening to us. If you are familiar with the science of NLP (Neuro Linguistic Programming) you will know that we don't even notice the majority of things that happen around us. But those things that we do notice have an impact on the choices we make during the course of our lives.

There are certain things that happen around us that we can control, like the people we choose to associate with or the actions we choose to take. There are also certain things that happen around us that we cannot control, such as the weather, the opinions of other people or the fact that (in the UK at least) we are required to pay income tax. Whether we can control what happens around us or not, it is an absolute fact that the one thing we can (and must learn to) control is our attitude to what happens around us.

So, if we cannot always choose what happens around us where does choice come into attitude control? Good question ("Thanks, well done me."). The answer is in the next step in our diagram.

YOU give it a meaning.

This is the point of choice. As soon as something, anything, happens to us we give it a meaning. We have to. As human beings we are meaning making machines. Listen to yourself and others over the next twenty-four hours and see how many times you, or someone else, says "You know what that means don't you?" It is at this point that you decide whether to respond or to react.

Let's look at an example. Two people are on a golf course when it starts to rain heavily. Both of them run off the course towards the clubhouse. One is cursing because the weather has spoilt their day out and the other is laughing … because they are a taxi driver. And everyone wants a taxi when it is raining.

Another one could involve two people in a vehicle that is stuck in traffic. The driver is becoming very frustrated at the delay because it will make him late for a dinner appointment with his partner. The passenger however is very pleased at the delay because it will make him very late for dinner with his partner. The driver's partner is his girlfriend and tonight he plans to propose marriage. However the passenger's partner is his cellmate in the prison he is returning to.

One other example could be the much-told story of the two shoe salespeople who went to darkest Africa. When they arrived both sent a fax back to their office. The first fax read: "No one here wears shoes, trip a disaster, bring me home." The second one however sent a fax that read: "No one here wears shoes, could be a profitable trip, send me one thousand pairs."

In all three cases the situation that occurred was exactly the same for both parties. The twist was that in all three cases one part saw a positive in the situation whilst the other saw a negative. In each case it was the same occurrence but with two completely different meanings. **Choice!** What a wonderful word don't you think?

YOU react to YOUR meaning.

So, now you have given whatever happened a meaning, your reaction can be based only upon that meaning. Therefore, you can never again say that something else annoyed you, made you angry or just generally wound you up, because it, or they, didn't. The meaning you gave to whatever happened is what wound you up. Ipso facto (cool expression don't you think?) If you don't like your reaction to something or to someone, change the meaning you give to it. And it really is as simple as that.

Your reaction becomes a habit.

If you find yourself getting wound up every time you hit slow moving or stationary traffic it won't be too long before you find the same negative reaction just by seeing a set of brake lights coming on in front of you.

However, if you decide to give a positive meaning to the things that happen to you, you will very quickly get into the habit of finding something positive in just about everything. Then you can join me and the other tree huggers in our journey through life. It's not that difficult really, and the good thing is that it really gets up the noses of the pessimists of the world when you won't join them in their "let's ban everything just in case," rants.

Your habits form your attitude.

So here we are. We have taken what has happened to us and chosen to give it a positive slant (meaning). This has caused us to have a positive reaction, which in turn has contributed to our positive attitude. And so we embark on our "hairy fairy," "unrealistic," "head in the clouds," or just "too positive to be real" existence. But it will astound you how well your life turns out once you have decided to look on the bright side. Positive people will want to be around you. An even better result though is that negative people will not want to be around you. They will tell you that you are "just no fun any more." How cool is that?

Make a note here of the person or the situation that you are no longer going to give your permission to annoy you. How will you choose to react instead?

> *No one can make you feel inferior*
> *Without your consent*
> *Eleanor Roosevelt*

Maintaining a positive attitude.

So there you have it. You have decided to become a positive person by choosing to give everything a positive meaning. Now, as we have already discussed, all you have to do is protect yourself from those whose very existence you threaten - the **outboard motors**. Here is a short reminder of what an outboard motor is.
Outboard motors:

Easily identifiable by the way they walk around all day going but, but, but, but!!

Believe You Can

Outboard motors are the people who don't mind having a bad day (in fact they quite enjoy it) as long as you have a bad day too.

Have you got that cold that's going around?

Have you noticed how the new guy in sales really winds you up?

Isn't the weather today miserable?
(Note: To outboard motors the weather is a never ending source of negativity. It is always too cold, too hot, muggy, miserable or "not nearly as nice as it was this time last year.")

These are just some of the ways that the outboards will attempt to hijack your positive attitude. Be aware but do not be afraid. If you show fear they will pounce. On the other hand if you stand firm and give them a positive answer they will run off with their propeller between their legs and find another outboard to give them some sympathy.

Just tell them, out loud if necessary:

"You do not have my permission to annoy me!"

To maintain your positive attitude it might first help to know what a positive attitude is, and what it isn't. Let's cover the latter first. A positive attitude is not walking around with a permanent grin on your face 'pretending' to be happy all of the time. Neither is it waking up every morning and shouting, "Hello world I feel fantastic and it's great to be alive!" In truth, saying all of that stuff, on occasions, is just telling a pack of lies. And a positive attitude does not mean that you believe that everything you attempt in your life is going to go well or finish perfectly.

Having a positive attitude does not mean that you can be brilliant at everything you attempt. My good friend Barrie is a rugby league prop forward who has represented Great Britain on several occasions. You know the type, muscles in his spit, two hundred and

34

fifty pounds, strong as an ox and if he says it's Friday, it's Friday. Barrie is a winner who gives one hundred percent to everything he does. However, I am convinced that Barrie would make the world's worst professional jockey. But put him on a horse next to a five stone weakling who doesn't think he can ride and my money will be on big Baz.

A positive attitude is about more than just the thoughts you have. It is more to do with the way you approach life in general. It involves, as we have already discussed, focussing on the positive rather than the negative in any given situation. It involves looking for the good in people before you underline the bad. A positive attitude means thinking well of yourself and treating yourself well, avoiding putting yourself down when things go less than perfectly.

A positive attitude means speaking to yourself with respect and never saying anything to yourself that, if someone else said it, would offend you. It means trusting people to treat you well and not to rip you off at the first opportunity. Having a positive attitude means that you are prepared to accept that sometimes things could have gone better (outboard motors would say "things go wrong") but accepting that there is learning to be done and that a solution is available, even if you don't know what or where it is. In short ladies and gentlemen, having a positive attitude means *looking* for the good in everything and everybody but not being upset or angry if you don't always find it.

Here are a few things that you can do to maintain your positive attitude:

I guess the first thing you could do is wake up every morning and shout "It's a fantastic day and I'm glad to be alive!" We know though that this will not be enough and, as I have found out from experience, it will most probably get on the nerves of anyone within listening distance, so don't do it. If you upset the people you live and sleep with you are in for an uphill struggle from the start. You could wake up and think it though.

Believe You Can

Have a plan for the day or the week.
Have you ever sat down at the end of the day and said something like "I've run around like a headless chicken all day and done nothing?"

That won't do a great deal to maintain a positive attitude. If you start your day, or your week, with a list of things that you will have accomplished by the close of play, you will be able to look back at the finish and say, "Well done me." Personally, I have a weekly sheet (only one A4 sheet) of things other than work related jobs which, if I get them done, will let me know I have had a productive week. I am always amazed by the amount of work I get done, sometimes without realising it, by the end of the week. AND I watch less rubbish on the television.

Play the re-frame game.
Re-framing is quite simply taking an seemingly negative situation and looking, sometimes very deeply, for a positive meaning within it. And it is possible to find something positive in everything. It may not be immediately apparent though what that positive thing is. On my web site at ***www.clivegott.com*** I have written a whole story about the five or six worst things that have ever happened to me in my life between March of 1986 and May of 2002. On each occasion I was convinced that this was THE worst thing that had ever happened to me. They include suffering a major injury to my knee and consequently having to give up my career as a fire fighter, losing my driving licence, which threatened my job, and being accused of racism, resulting in the loss of a lucrative contract just after I had started my own business. However in retrospect every one of those incidents, and the others mentioned in the story, happened for a reason. I did not realise at the time but when I look back at when they happened and what followed as a result I realise that I would not be enjoying the life I am leading right now (I am leading the life I always dreamed of leading) if any of these things had never happened.

How does this help you might ask? Well nowadays when something goes decidedly pear shaped, as it sometimes still does, I am well aware that whatever it is has happened for a very good reason. If that reason is not immediately apparent I know *for a fact* that something positive will come out of it, it is just a matter of looking for it.

Be aware of the law of association.
Take a look at the person immediately to your left do they look ok? Now take a look at the person to your right and check them over.

Apparently one in three people in the world is unstable, if those two look all right you might be in trouble.

Someone once told me that "in ten years time you will be a reflection of whatever you are reading and the people you are associating with today." Seriously this time, take a look around you. Do the people you are associating with reflect the kind of person you want to become? It is an absolute fact that we are a reflection of our surroundings. The creatures of the forest and jungle have a gift. They can change themselves to blend into their surroundings; they have to in order to protect themselves.

The challenge is that if an animal feels threatened by being in the jungle it can't just waltz off and live in the city. Only we humans have the ability to change our surroundings to match the life we want to live.

Take a moment to ask yourself this question, "Are the people I am following (or associating with) going where I want to go?" If not I strongly suggest that you change the people you are following or associating with. There is a saying that 'pigs don't know that pigs stink.' They hang around with each other day in and day out, so they don't notice. Well the same goes for people. Negative people don't know they are negative because they probably spend their time with negative people.

Why not spring clean your address book. If you don't want to go to the part with the outboards, *don't go!* It really is as simple as that.

Believe You Can

Don't worry about your old associates, they won't miss you for long and you won't be on your own for long either. Buy a personal development book, something like "Unlimited Power" by Anthony Robins. Sit in public and read it. You will be amazed at the people who will start a conversation with you. (You will also be amazed at how many times you see that book on the shelves now but that's another chapter.) Oh you might miss the old outboards for a while, and they you. But it won't be too long before you are engrossed in your new social circle and they are saying things like "What happened to Mary?" "Oh her, she is one of those tree huggers now, always got her nose in some woo woo book (outboard speak for personal development) and talking about that goal setting c**p." The amazing thing is though that when you start to achieve your goals of better relationships, great job, nice house and driving the car of your dreams, the outboards will justify their continued mediocrity by deciding that you were "lucky."

I believe the whole thing is summed up by a fantastic quote from my good friend Steve McDermott's book "How to be a complete and utter failure in work life and everything." The quote simply says:

"If you wish to know your past life look at your present circumstances. If you wish to know your future look at your present actions."

A few short suggestions to help maintain a positive attitude:

Learn to accept a compliment. Just say "Thank you."

Keep a journal. Put all of the good stuff in there like some of your bigger goals (use pictures), thank you cards and the like. Write a list of your favourite things and another of your life's achievements.

Do some exercise and get that weight off. Healthy body, healthy mind, you know the score. Gaining weight is not an accident. Between 1982 and 1986 I gained over seven stone in weight. In all of that time I can never recall *accidentally* eating anything. Neither was it an accident when I lost it all again and, for the most part, kept it off.

Send a thank you card at least once a week. This forces you to look for something to be grateful for instead of looking for something to complain about.

Wake up every morning and shout out "It's a fantastic day and I'm happy to be alive." Oh no, we said we weren't going to do that didn't we? How about thinking it then.

Write a list out right now of everything you know for a fact that you have to look forward to over the coming months. If you don't have anything to put on your list book a weekend away *NOW* so that you do have something to look forward to.

Set some goals. We will talk later about goal setting but for now just write down a few small things that you would like to achieve over the next week or so. Nothing too fancy or testing (yet anyway), just a few small things that perhaps you have been putting off for some time. You will be pleasantly surprised by how motivated and focused you become just by writing them down.

Adopt a positive habit. Identify some of the negative things you do or say simply by force of habit and change them to more positive actions or words. Perhaps you have a habit of waking up on a morning and saying "I'm tired" or "I **have** to get up." Maybe you are in the habit of saying, "I've **got** to go to work." You haven't **got** to go to work, you **get** to go to work.

Do you go to places that make you feel less than positive or hang around people who have the same effect? If so change your habits, hang around with different people and in different places.

Just take a few minutes to identify some of the negative habits you have or some of the negative things you say to yourself, again by force of habit. Focus for a day on noticing what it is you say or do, or who it is that makes you feel less than positive. Accept that it is *your* habit that makes you feel this way. And then change your habit.

The first new positive habit you could adopt is to develop a positive greeting. When someone asks you how you are right now, how do you answer? OK, not bad, compared to what, fine considering, fair to mediocre, are just some of the negative replies I have heard in response to the question. Those people who really know me will know that my personal greeting is a little more positive than any of the examples given here. Whenever I am asked how I am my reply is **always** the same ... "Fantastic thanks, how are you?" It takes just as long to say and makes me feel better every time I say it. The chances are that the person or persons I am saying it to will feel a little better too, and they will think a little more about their response. Another positive spin off from a response like this is that if you say it to an outboard they may well come back with a response like "What have you got to feel fantastic about?" This will give you an opportunity to tell them, and to remind yourself, just exactly what it is that makes you feel so good about life. "Thanks for asking. I have a fantastic life. I have a wonderful family and a beautiful home. I haven't got to do my job, I get to do my job. I am fit and healthy. I have a beautiful wife and an independent, confident daughter. I have a social circle that I am more than happy with. I have a series of goals that stimulate and excite me. I believe that if it is raining it is making my garden look so much better for me to sit in when it is fine and sunny. I understand that where I go and what I do in my life will be as a result of the choices that I make. Shall I go on?"

Don't worry if some of these sound a little hairy fairy even for you. The majority of outboard motors will have left you alone as soon as you said "thanks for asking." No doubt they will have walked away from you whispering something about your mental state and your inability to see the 'real world.' You might even be privileged enough to be called "*unrealistic.*" You know you are becoming the best you can possibly be when the outboards refer to you as

---

unrealistic. That is their cop out word for "I know it's possible but I really can't be bothered." I won't go there but I could write a whole chapter on the word realistic. Just accept that it is not a word that people in our woo woo land use; it's a cop out for not giving anything and everything your very best.

> *"The greatest discovery of my generation is that a human being can change their life by altering their attitude of mind."*
> ### *William James*

Develop a positive anchor. There will be times when the outboards will sing out with glee because they have finally brought you down to their level. They have proved that you are fallible. They can run around the workplace or wherever telling everyone that you are not always the positive person you claim to be and that *they* are the ones who made you snap. And unfortunately they could be right. However, you might sometimes feel less than positive for some other reason. Sometimes your reason might not even be apparent, you just don't feel like it today. What if you *have to* feel positive and be up? What if you are a teacher or a speaker or a sports star? What if this is your biggest public speech of the year or worse still the Olympic final (or your equivalent) and for one reason or another you just don't feel like it. What then?

Quite frankly I don't think it is possible to be up at the top all day and every day. I think that even the most positive person is going to feel a little negative at some point. Let's look at our possible attitudes on a scale of one to ten. Here is our *Mood Scale*:

- **10 = Cloud cuckoo land. Up there with the woo woo people**
- **9**
- **8**
- **7**
- **6**
- **5 = Really don't care much. A bit of a Pooh Bear**
- **4**
- **3**
- **2**
- **1 = Fully paid up member of the outboard motor club**

As you can see, even I don't think that living your life at a constant ten is at all possible, or even good for you. Neither is living at a constant one. And poor old Pooh Bear there in the middle, well he doesn't know if he is drilled, bored or countersunk. And quite frankly he doesn't care. Our Pooh Bears by the way can sometimes be more dangerous than even the worst outboard. At least the outboards know what they want. The one in the middle can be swayed either way depending on whoever or whatever is the strongest influence at the time. But they don't particularly stand for anything. And as someone infinitely more clever than me once said:

If you don't stand for something
You will fall for anything.

Ideally we should be looking to spend the majority of our lives around the seven to nine mark. That leaves us a little to play with on the days when we feel way up there and need some room in the clouds. The danger though is that it also leaves plenty of room below us for when the going gets a little tough. So how do we get back up on those inevitable times when we drop below six or five and leave ourselves vulnerable to the Pooh Bears and the outboards? The answer is *we develop an anchor*.

What is an anchor? If you think about it literally, an anchor is something that keeps something else fixed to a particular spot, like a ship's anchor.   However if you think about it in a personal development sense an anchor is something that, when applied at

Peak State, will act as a constant reminder of that state and bring us back to that state when it is applied. If this was an NLP (Neuro Linguistic Programming) book we would spend pages here talking about anchors and how to develop them, collapse them, chain them and so on. But it's not, so we won't. We will just discuss, simply, what an anchor is and how to develop one for yourself.

Firstly let me explain what I mean by peak state. At any time of the day or night you will be in a state, a place of being. A state can be described I guess as how you are feeling at any given time. Sleep is a state as is love, anger, and frustration. Happy, sad, elated, hate, relaxed, tense, these are all states that we can get ourselves into. Or we can allow someone else to get us into if we are not vigilant with our attitude.   Peak state is when you are at the height of any particular state. Peak state is not just being angry it is being *really* angry. Being at your peak in a relaxed state is not just 'chillin' it is being almost horizontal. Peak state is not just being somewhere, it is *really* being somewhere. An outside stimulus such as music, or a smell or a touch can very easily be turned into an anchor when applied in this state. The dodgy thing about anchors being applied like this though is that someone else can also apply them to you, without you even realising it, like a disc jockey at a dance or nightclub. You must have heard of the "our song syndrome?" This is when you only have to hear a particular piece of music to be reminded of a time when you were perfectly happy or not as the case may be.   This would be referred to as an *auditory* anchor. How about a smell? Newly mown grass or freshly baked bread might take you straight back to your childhood. This is known as an *olfactory* anchor. Likewise you might be returned to a time when you were in peak state just by seeing something or someone, it could be someone you either love or indeed you dislike intently. Perhaps it is someone who has upset you deeply in the past or someone you have loved deeply in your past (or even right now). Just seeing that person or even a picture of that person can change you from the state you are

Believe You Can

in right now back to the state you were in when the anchor was applied. This is known as a *visual* anchor. And then there is a touch. If you only need to feel someone or something touching you

in a particular place or in a particular way to remind you of a time when you were *really* in a particular state, that would be known as a *kinaesthetic* anchor. All of these anchors can be applied to you by someone else without you knowing and most of the time at least, without them knowing either.

The good news is that you can also consciously create your own anchors that will serve you in a positive way when you need them. Personally I respond well to auditory anchors. I have two particular pieces of music that whenever I hear them they serve as positive anchors and help me to feel successful and fantastic. Whether I am delivering a forty-five minute key-note speech or a five-day training programme I will always play one of the pieces of music prior to delivery of my talk or programme. It doesn't matter which piece, either works just as well. I will do the same if I have chosen to attend a meeting or gathering that I am feeling less than enthusiastic about when I get there. There is one other piece of music that makes the hairs stand up on the back of my neck. This anchor was applied in India in 2003. I was part of a team that delivered a three-day conference to a group of around four hundred delegates. At the start of each session and at the end of the conference the same piece of music was used. The conference was a resounding success and therefore, whenever I hear that piece of music, I am taken straight back to a time in my career when many other people and I were in a peak state of success.

That is my round about way of telling you that you too should create an anchor for yourself to take you back 'up there' when you find yourself dropping below six or five on our one-to-ten attitude scale. It doesn't have to be a piece of music, that might take too long to listen to or, worse still, you might not have the facilities to play it. What about a short positive statement? Brian Tracy in his audio programme "The Psychology of Success" admits to saying the

44

statement "back to work, back to work" over and over again to himself. Sara (my wife) and I are great fans of the Al Pachino film "Scent of a Woman." We can often be heard saying, "ooh haaa" to make us both smile and feel positive (if you haven't seen the film

you won't have a clue what I am on about right now). Of course these are all auditory anchors. If these don't work for you then it is just a case of you deciding what would work for you. Perhaps you are a more kinaesthetic (touchy feely) person, in which case you will need an anchor that you can feel, like clapping your hands or clicking your fingers. An example of a visual anchor might be a picture, perhaps of your children, or of something that you would like to own one day. This sort of anchor would act as a reminder to you as to why you are doing what you are doing, why it is that you are working so hard.

So you see I don't really care what you decide to use as your positive anchor but for those times when you find yourself dropping below six or five on our scale, I do care that you have one. That way you can get back 'up there' as quickly as you possibly can. Remember that the longer you stay below six or five the more time those outboards have to work you over!

Developing unshakeable self-confidence

Developing unshakeable self-confidence.

Outboard motor's thoughts:
You can have all the self-confidence you want. But if someone wants to louse up your day and make you feel c*** they will do. And there is nothing you can do about it.

Author's thoughts:
Funnily enough I can empathise with our friends above and their thoughts on self-confidence. Speaking to yourself with respect is an excellent way to develop unshakeable self-confidence. And it might also be true that however confident you are there will always be someone who will try to break you. But in both cases, whether it is believing yourself when you talk yourself up, or whether it is succumbing to the negative attacks of the outboards, you will need your own permission to react in whatever way you choose.

Developing unshakeable self-confidence is not something you are going to do overnight. Let's think about the opposite of high self-confidence first and that, funnily enough, is low self-confidence. Where does low self-confidence come from? My guess is that it comes from a series of setbacks or perceived failures in your past. Perhaps you have tried something and it went terribly wrong. Whatever it was that didn't go to plan (wrong if you are and outboard) might have lost you money or worse still, it might have made you feel foolish in front of friends or family. I have worked with more than one person who has a fear of speaking in public purely because they once tried it and they forgot what they were going to say or someone laughed at them or said something less than complimentary. Perhaps you are one of those people who were constantly put down by friends or family. When you had those great big dreams that kids have, were you laughed at? Perhaps you were told you were too small, too weak, or too shy? All of these things can, and invariably will (if constantly repeated), destroy anyone's self-confidence. What happens then, because you have kept a concise record of every time something didn't go quite right, you refer to those references whenever you think about trying something new or challenging. Just by tapping into your failure files you will find all of the evidence you need to prevent you from even trying.

Well here is the good news. If you keep a record of everything you have ever done that you were successful at, or everything you have ever achieved in your life, you can use these as your success files. These files too can be referred to every time you need a little extra confidence to attempt something challenging or new.

Think about it, you know it makes sense. If every time you want to try something new just tapping into your failure files destroys your self-confidence, then surely tapping into your success files will have the opposite effect? Now here is the catch. Most of the people I work with can talk all day about the things they can't do or the things they have tried that didn't go to plan. But ask the same person to tell you about the things that they have achieved, therefore the things that they can do, and they will clam up tighter than an outboard motor's compliment file. And why do you think that is? Simply because most people see their achievements and victories as an expectation or "nothing special."

When I ask the people on my programmes to list all of their achievements there is usually someone who writes down "passed my exams." When I push them to tell us what exams or how many they will invariably tell us about their eight GCSE exams, the four 'A' levels and the masters degree they have achieved. Yet they refer to it as "passing some exams." Well excuse me but as someone who has to borrow a spirit level (I have no qualifications from my days of formal education) I happen to think passing any exam that requires study, revision, more study, more revision and finally, after about five years of this torture, sitting an examination, is something very special. If keeping a record of our "failures" destroys our self-confidence then surely keeping a record of our achievements, no matter how small someone else might think they are, *must* have the opposite effect.

My colleague Nigel Risner has people create a list of 501 of their achievements. Not a bad exercise but one that requires a great deal of confidence. So work your way up to 501 by starting with 52, one for every week of the last year. Then go back another year and keep going until you get to "learned to walk." You will soon have a fantastic list of your life's little victories to refer to when you need a little confidence. My reasons for encouraging you to create this list are simple. On the days when you don't think you can, you can look at your list and see what you did on the days when you knew that you could. If you can learn to walk, take a driving test, travel to Australia or pass your cycling proficiency test you can do ***anything you want to do***.

Impossible
is just
I'm possible
with something missing

Paint better pictures.

When you think about it confidence is the opposite of fear isn't it? So it might be pertinent to discuss for a few moments what fear is. There are many explanations of what fear is. One of my favourites is that "fear is a negative anticipation of the future."

Fear has also been described as negative goal setting. One of the most common explanations used by myself, and by my colleagues in the personal development field, is that fear is:

False		**Forget**
Evidence	(or even)	**Everything**
Appearing		**And**
Real		**Run**

49

Believe You Can

Most of the things we fear have never happened. Fear of failure has to be the greatest fear people suffer from today. Some people will never attempt anything because they are convinced that whatever it is will end up in failure. And the only proof they have is in the form of a picture created in their heads of what failure looks like. You can do it right now. Think of something you would like to attempt and create a picture in your head of what it would look like if the whole thing went belly up. How would you feel? What would you look like to your peers? What would people say to you, or worse still about you when you had finished making a complete fool of your self. I bet you can create a picture so vivid and perfect that you even feel embarrassed just thinking about it.

Fear of heights is another favourite. Someone who is afraid of heights has no evidence that should they climb to the top of a high building they will fall off. All they have is the evidence they have already created in their heads in the form of pictures. Likewise, the fear of flying. Other than the fact that an occasional aeroplane has crashed in the past what evidence does anyone who is afraid of flying have that *this particular aeroplane* is going to crash? The answer is none at all.

I am not ridiculing anyone's fears here. Fear is a seriously debilitating feeling that has cost some people dearly in the past. All fears are, at the time, very real indeed. How about this for a radical idea though? What if no one is afraid to do or even to try anything? What if the only thing they are afraid of is how they will look or feel if (or when!) whatever it is they are trying goes horribly wrong? What if people are not afraid of speaking in public? What if all they are afraid of is looking foolish in front of an audience. What if people are not afraid of heights? What if they are afraid of ending up in a pile of broken bones and blood at the bottom? (Here is a thought for you. How come no one is afraid of the ground? After all if you fall it is the ground that will kill you not the height!) What if the only thing people were afraid of are the pictures they paint in their heads?

Believe You Can

Now I can hear you outboard motors grumbling right now. "That's a ridiculous statement. If we were only afraid of the pictures we paint in our heads then all we have to do is create a better picture." **BINGO!!!!!** If you outboards keep thinking like that we will make tree huggers of you yet.

That's the answer isn't it? If all we are afraid of are the pictures we paint in our heads then why not just paint a better picture? If a lack of self-confidence is really only fear of failure, and the negative pictures that we paint in our heads bring about failure, then unshakeable self-confidence must be the result of creating positive pictures. After all, whether we are confident about an outcome or in fear of an outcome, we don't actually have any proof of our outcome until we achieve our outcome do we? (You might want to read all of that again, I did.)

So there you have it. We must all become Picassos of our own thoughts. Paint some nice pictures. Put the person you want to become right there in the middle of your first picture. Put the person, or the people, you want to spend the rest of your life with next to you in the picture. Have yourselves standing in front of your dream house with your dream car on the drive next to you. In fact put anything you want in the picture. After all that is all you have been doing when you have created fear about an outcome up to now.

If you have a fear of speaking in public create a picture of you delivering a fantastic presentation and of the audience giving you a resounding round of applause at the end. If you are having a meeting with someone, a client or a colleague at work (or the boss!) why not create a picture of how you will greet the person or persons. If it is a sales call create a picture of the client signing the order form. If you are driving home from work create a picture of how you will greet you partner or your kids when you walk through the door. If you have created any sort of fear for yourself in the past you have done it by creating pictures. It's how we all think, in pictures. So if you have to think in pictures you might as well make them good, positive pictures of the outcomes you will look forward to instead of fear.

Empowering or limiting belief systems

What are beliefs?

Outboard motor's thoughts:

"They are lies you tell yourself to make you feel good. My beliefs have always been taken from me though. They are not true and you shouldn't rely on them. If it was just as easy as believing something I would believe I was a millionaire wouldn't I? Do you think I actually want to live this life like I do? The fact is I was put here to do a job and that is all I will ever be able to do. Anyway, what right do I have to believe I can be more than my parents were? If it was good enough for them it has to be good enough for me!"

Author's thoughts:

Everything our outboard has said above is true. Why? Simple, he believes it to be true. I have met countless people who agree with him. Crikey I used to agree with him myself, until one day I chose to challenge one of my beliefs and then another and then another. In the space of four years I went from a grossly overweight fire-fighter to an accomplished athlete who could run a marathon at will and complete an Ironman triathlon (2.5 mile swim 112 mile cycle, and a 26.2 mile run) in a little over nine and a half hours (once anyway).

You see up to that point I believed that I was stuck with who I was, what I was and where I was. I too thought that I was a part of some higher authority's master plan. But then I started to challenge some of those beliefs. Did I have to do this because my parents did? Do I have to go here because it is where people from my town go? Do I have to do this job because I am not capable of doing anything else? And surprisingly enough the answer to all of those questions was a great big resounding *no*.

So to answer the original question: "What is a belief?" A belief is merely something we accept as true. And our beliefs are often based on our emotions rather that facts. For example, if you are going to a gathering of some sort, perhaps a party or a wedding, or if you are in business perhaps a networking meeting, and you believe that everyone you are about to meet are really very nice people. The chances are that you will have a great time and meet lots of nice people. The reason being that you will attend the gathering and look for reasons to justify your beliefs. However, if your beliefs, and therefore your expectations, are completely the opposite, then your results too will be opposite. And your initial information about the people you were about to meet probably came from someone else who had met these people previously.

The same can apply when you go on holiday. If you tell someone you are going to a particular place and that you are feeling very excited about going because you expect it to be a wonderful experience, they might change your beliefs by telling you that they travelled there last year and had the worst holiday ever. Their opinions could change your expectations of what you will experience and so change the whole outcome of your holiday. In short, once we have internalised a belief it will re-present itself to us as a feeling of absolute certainty.

I heard a startling fact recently from a psychologist friend of mine. She told me that when a jury in a criminal trial sees the defendant for the first time they are likely to make up their minds as to whether the defendant is guilty or not in the first few minutes. They may then spend the rest of the trial justifying their initial decision. How many times have you done that with a person or a place? When was the last time you made an initial decision based on first impressions and then looked for ways to justify your decision?

If you are serious about changing some of your outcomes in life and achieving a great deal more for yourself and for those around you, then perhaps this would be as good a place as any to decide to make changes. Might I suggest that you start to take notice of some of your beliefs, perhaps by noticing some of your expectations of people or situations around you? If your present results or behaviours are not what you desire then the chances are that you are on your way to identifying a limiting belief that you hold about yourself. At this point it might be a good idea to explore some of the origins of our present beliefs.

Where do our beliefs come from?

We don't have to look too far for the origins of our first set of beliefs. Most of them will have come from *your parents* or at least your environment. It is worth pointing out that the beliefs we were given by our parents were probably given with the very best of intentions, to protect you from something that they believed would, or could, do you harm. How many of you were told that if you swallow chewing gum it would wrap around your heart and kill you? Now I don't think our parents actually believed that, but by telling it to us they would stop us swallowing our gum. Something they know was not good for us but they were not too sure why it was not good for us.

The bogeyman, the Easter bunny, Father Christmas, are all beliefs that were given to us at some point to serve a purpose. Most of these beliefs were corrected at some point in our lives but some others perhaps are still accounting for some of the decisions we make today.

Our past results will also have a strong bearing on our present beliefs. Have you tried something in the past that didn't work only to adopt a belief that you "can't do it?" Perhaps you tried something at school only to be told by a teacher that you were silly, or worse still, as was the case with me, that you would never amount to anything?

Knowledge will have an influence on your beliefs. Not knowing how to do something does not mean that you have to adopt a belief that you can't do it. This one goes hand in hand with our past results. If we attempt something and it doesn't work, losing weight or saving money are common situations that might involve our 'failing', we adopt a belief of "I tried but I can't."

Here is a question that is a little radical I know but nevertheless worth asking. What if some of the beliefs you hold about yourself and your abilities, or at least you have held until now, no longer serve your purpose? What if you decided to change some of your beliefs because holding on to them is holding you back?

What if you could actually choose what you believe about yourself?

The truth is that you can. And get this, the more vivid your self-belief the more you will come to accept it. Have you ever believed that you were going to be late, and you were? Have you ever believed that a party or a gathering of some kind, was going to be a let down, and it was? Have you ever believed that you could lose weight but that you would just put it all back on again, and you did? Have you ever believed that although your relationship is going really well right now, as usual something will happen to spoil it, and it does? If none of these suits you think of your own. We all have them. They are called limiting beliefs.

Here is the good news. If you can believe any or all of the above and be proved correct then you can believe completely the opposite of all of the above and be proved completely correct. Whatever limiting beliefs you have you can change them into empowering beliefs just by changing your thoughts.

Now I'm not saying that golfers, by changing their thoughts from "watch me put this in the bunker" (limiting belief) to "watch me get a hole in one" (empowering belief), will indeed get a hole in one every time. But they will spend a lot less time in the rough. And so will you when you change your limiting beliefs into empowering beliefs. But first we have to identify our beliefs. Having done this we can then decide whether a particular belief is serving us positively or negatively. You are not going to do this over night. We have thousands of beliefs. But we can start right now. Try this exercise.

What would you really like to do but can't?

Let's leave the world changing events for a while and start on something simple. What small thing have you been putting off because you believe that you either can't do it or dare not do it? Write it down here along with the reason why you can't or dare not do it. Make it simple. Perhaps it is just a phone call. Or it could be taking some exercise or booking a holiday. You may have been putting off opening a savings account because you have tried saving in the past and something always happens to take your savings. Or volunteering to give a presentation at wok for fear of looking silly. Whatever it is write it down here.

I have been putting off:

Because:

Now let's take a little time to identify the belief that is holding you back from taking some positive action. Let's also look at the origins of that belief.

The limiting belief I have is:

This belief originated from:

Now let's look at what holding on to this limiting belief will cost you.

Believe You Can

If I continue to embrace this belief I will never be able to:

And that will mean:

Our next step is to start looking at the positive reasons for changing our limiting belief.

If I decide to change this limiting belief I will be able to:

And that will mean:

Fantastic! Now for the big step. What new empowering belief, if you adopted it, would serve you best in achieving whatever it is you have been putting off? Write it down as an empowering personalised belief that will serve you positively. For example, "I believe that, given time to prepare, I can deliver a professional presentation to my colleagues." Or "I believe that if I take professional advice I can start to build a savings fund for my future." Even "I believe that I am worthy of a loving and lasting relationship with my ideal partner. I also believe that my ideal partner is out there somewhere." Write out an empowering belief that you could adopt if you choose to, and that will serve you well.

An empowering belief I would like to have about myself is:

Now all we need to concern ourselves with is how. And we will cover that later in the chapter on goal setting. But for now you should be congratulating yourself for taking a massive step towards creating a series of empowering beliefs that will move you towards the success that you truly desire, and away from the perceived failure that you don't want.

Developing core beliefs.

Core beliefs are the same as ordinary beliefs except that they are *none negotiable*. Most of my beliefs are a little like my car. I am more than happy with my car right now, it serves its purpose and meets my needs. I have no intention of changing my car for a few years, why should I? After all, as I say, it meets my needs. However if some very clever car salesman worked his patter on me, and I was feeling a little vulnerable at the time, I might just be convinced to change it. Most of my beliefs are like that. But my core beliefs are *none negotiable*. I will not be persuaded to change them under any circumstances.

My three core beliefs not only serve me very well they also protect me from some of the outboards. They keep me on track when I am feeling less than positive or energetic. In short, at the times when I really need them, they could well be my best friends. It might be pertinent at this point to share with you my three core beliefs. They are:

1. **My wife Sara and I will be together forever.**

2. **Anything is possible if you are committed enough.**

3. **Someone somewhere wants to do business with me.**

Believe You Can

Now these beliefs might now work for you. So I suggest that you refrain from rushing out telling people that you believe you will be together with Clive's wife Sara forever, or that you firmly believe that someone somewhere wants to do business with Clive. You see the beauty of MY core beliefs is that they are just that, MY core beliefs. And here is the interesting bit, - I don't even know if they are true. In fact I know that at least one of them is a down right lie. I honestly don't think I could walk from my house to my friend Charlie's house in Perth Australia in a week. But if necessary I would give it my best shot.

Let's take a closer look at my third core belief: someone somewhere wants to do business with me. As well as designing and delivering my material I have to sell all of my own material. Now I know that some of you will find this hard to understand but there are some people and organisations out there who actually don't want to work with me. In fact there are more than I can count. But there are enough people and organisations out there that do want to work with me to keep my busy until the day I choose to turn my attentions to the next chapter in my life. (Outboard motors call this retiring.) Unfortunately I am not able to make the distinction until I ask them for business. And sometimes lots of those who don't want to work with me come along together. (Outboards call this rejection.) When they do, I need something to keep me focussed on the fact that there is plenty of work out there. Enter core belief number three.

So how about you? If you had a core belief, a belief that would serve you well and protect you from some of the negative situations that you might face, what would it be? What one belief, if you had it, would motivate you to go that little further in the pursuit of your dreams? Let's have a play.

Believe You Can

One core belief I would like to adopt is:

Remember here that when you write this belief down you don't even have to believe it ... but what if you did? Write down your core belief and then try it out for a week or so. Say it over and over again to yourself. Tell someone close to you that this is what you believe. I found it helped enormously when I shared my number one core belief with Sara. Look for situations when you can use your belief and then shout out "See, I told me so!" when you are proved correct. It is amazing how quickly you will adopt your belief as fact. And when the outboards start to challenge your beliefs, as they invariably will, with questions like "How do you know?" remember what John Nash, a world famous mathematician, said in the film Beautiful Minds. His fiancé asked him how big the universe is. He replied, "It is infinite." She said, "How do you know?" His reply was "because all of the data proves it to be." To which she replied "But how do you REALLY know?" John Nash, one of the greatest mathematicians ever, replied, "I don't, I just believe it to be so." Your core beliefs are the same. You don't need proof, you just need to believe it to be so.

Whether you believe you can
or you believe you cannot
you are absolutely right
                    Henry Ford

Developing and maintaining motivation

or

"I would if I could but I can't be bothered."

What is Motivation?

Outboard motor's thoughts:

"Motivation, that's when you get on with what you have to do because we damn well have to pay the bills and raise our kids. I wish I had the luxury of being motivated or not but I don't. I **have** to go to work everyday. **I don't have a choice**. Don't you think that if it was just a case of motivating myself I would be a lot happier than I am now?"

Author's thoughts:

Hmmm! An interesting outlook. Our friend has just described a type of motivation alien to the most successful people today, and that is motivation by fear. Our friend the outboard is motivated by fear of not paying the bills or not being able to raise and support the family. Outboard motors are motivated away from their perception of failure. Motivating yourself this way will always ensure that you are moving away from something you don't want to happen, in this case not paying bills or feeding the family.

Before we go any further let's take a look at what the word motivation means. If we break it down into two words **Motiv** (in this case without the 'e') and **Ation**. If you look in the Collins English dictionary **Motive** is explained as "a reason to." And according to ancient readings, **Ation** comes from the Latin for "action." Therefore, **motivation** means **"a reason to take action."** I can hear you all now. "If only it was that simple." If all you needed was a reason to take action then everyone who "feels fat" would have a reason to lose weight. Everyone who is "fed up with not being in a happy relationship" would have a reason to be happy. Anyone who is "frustrated with never having any money" would be motivated to earn more money. And people who were "dreading going to work on Monday" would easily be motivated to get themselves a job that they did look forward to going to. **"If only it was that easy"** I hear you cry. Well although it might not be "that simple," as you so eloquently put it, it (motivation) isn't really all that difficult. All you need is a better understanding of what it is and isn't.

What motivation is not:
Effective motivation (a reason to take action) is not just about having a reason to take action. We all have those. It is not just about getting to a place where you can no longer stand your present position or the outcomes you are achieving right now. Neither is it a series of threats of something negative that will happen if things don't change.

"If you don't work harder then you won't be here long?"

"I have to lose weight because I can't get into my favourite ... "

"If we don't work at our relationship we will end up divorced."

"If I don't save money I might have to work until I am 70."

I'm sure you can add loads of your own daily used expressions to this list. All of these expressions *are* motivating statements of a sort. They will all bring about some action. The challenge is though that they are negative statements and all are, in some way, ambiguous. Living your life by constantly reacting to statements like these will only ensure that you are always moving *away from* things that you don't want. They do not give you anything pleasurable to move *towards*. Written as positive statements using towards motivation they would look like this:

"If you work hard you can gain promotion and a salary increase."

"When I weigh (?) I can wear any clothes I choose to."

"Working together means we will be together forever."

"When I have savings of (?) I can choose when I work until."

Believe You Can

What is towards and away from motivation?

In short we are motivated by one of two things. We are either motivated towards pleasure or away from pain. That's it. There is no more. It really is as simple as that.

Actually it isn't just as simple as that. If it was we would all be doing it wouldn't we? But the principles really are that simple. If we want to stop doing something we have decided is not helping our development, or start doing something that will help our development, we must make the pain of doing nothing and the pleasure of moving forward so great that we would find it impossible to stay where we are.

In the past I have gone so deep in my explanations of these principles that even I have had trouble understanding what I am saying. So for the purposes of this book I am going to make my explanations as simple as possible. To help in my explanation I am going to use the analogy of a mountain and three types of mountaineers. *Quitters, Campers* and *Climbers.*

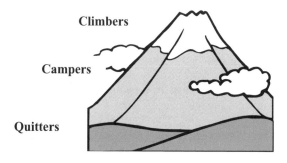

Imagine that whatever it is you are trying to motivate yourself to do is a mountain. At the base of the mountain, base camp, is the object, occurrence or present result that you want to motivate yourself to move away from. For ease of explanation I will use an example of having a goal to reduce either excess weight or debt. My guess is that most of you have had a goal to achieve one, or both of these at some point in your past. Perhaps you are even hoping this book will help you with them right now? My guess is also that if you have attempted to reduce either of these in the past you have been successful to a point and then, at the point of relaxation, you have found yourself going straight back to where you were. Or at least very close? You know the score. You go on a diet and lose 20 pounds. Then you say to yourself "I'm happy now so I will start eating sensibly again to keep the weight off." Only to watch it all go back on again, give or take a few pounds. Or, if your goal is financial, you get to a point where you are almost out of debt and then something happens that means you have to spend some money that you perhaps don't have only to find yourself back where you started. And you find it happening with monotonous regularity. (By the way, if you find yourself moving in and out of relationships with the same monotonous regularity, the same principles probably apply to you too.) So much so that you are ready to resign yourself to the beliefs that "Maybe I just have a natural body weight that I can't change?" Or "Maybe I am just one of those people who is destined never to have any money?" Or worse still "Perhaps I am destined to spend my life alone?" To accept this would make you a *Quitter*. And if you were a quitter you wouldn't be reading this book. So smile, pat yourself on the back, and read on.

Here is a startling fact that could well change your life, it certainly changed mine when I discovered it. *If you are not happy with who, what or where you are you can change it*. It is just a case of knowing how to change it.

Anyway, back to base camp. This is where you are when you are no longer willing to tolerate a weight gain or a debt. Different people have different tolerances. Personally my weight tolerance is based on my ability to stand on some scales and see fifteen stones and seven pounds or less. If I found myself over that weight I would immediately set a goal to move away from where I was. The same will happen with you, and whether you realise it or not, this is what you do. Perhaps yours is not an actual weight. Your measure might be a dress size or trouser waist size that you cannot fit into. Whatever it is this will be your point of zero tolerance. Once you hit your point of zero tolerance, and to avoid becoming a quitter, you will take steps and start climbing the mountain to move away from where you are. This is *away from* motivation. Used in this way, away from motivation is very powerful but only until you are far enough up the mountain that you can no longer see where, or what, it is that you don't want. At this point, because you are not using towards motivation, you will break out the tent and set up camp on the mountainside. You have now become a *Camper*!

The challenge with campers is that they are predominantly away from motivated people. A further challenge with predominantly away from motivated people is that although they are very clear about what it is they don't want, they are seldom as clear about what it is they *do* want. So when they are far enough away from whatever it is they don't want they strike up camp and stop moving at all. And when it comes to personal development there is no 'stood still'. We are either improving or getting worse, there is no stood still. Campers will find themselves starting a lot of sentences with the words "at least I"because they are not too sure of what it is they want they are usually happy just to move away from whatever it is that they don't want. Although they may not be completely satisfied with where they are, they will attempt to justify their present position by claiming, "It could be worse, at least I'm not as bad as some!" Or "At least I'm not as far in debt as I was." Even something like "It may not be a perfect relationship but at least I'm not alone!" Campers know that they could have so much more than they already have but to get it would take so much mere effort or risk so why rock the boat. After all "at least I'm not as bad as some people!"

So is away from motivation negative motivation?
Of course not. Away from motivation, used effectively, can act as a very powerful catalyst for getting us started in achieving our goals. Once we are aware of the minimum we will tolerate using away from motivation will start us on our journey to the success we desire. But as we have already explained, it will only work until we are far

enough up the mountain to make base camp a spot in the distance. And then we camp. It is at this point that we should start to turn our away from motivation into *towards* motivation. We have to become *Climbers*.

To become a climber is relatively simple. What you do is, as soon as you have reached a point where you can no longer see whatever it is that you don't want, you must then start to visualise what it is that you *do* want. This will then give us a focus to move towards. Let me explain using our old friends: weight loss and financial goals.

Setting a goal to either lose weight or pay off your debts is not just about setting away from goals. Goals to lose weight or pay off debts are negative goals (we will discuss the perils of this in a later chapter on goal setting). Think about it. If you have a goal to lose weight, what do you need to be before you can achieve your goal? Overweight, that's what. And if you have a goal to pay off your debts what do you need before you can achieve your goal? Debts, that's what. Using only away from motivation like this will ensure that you never achieve your goals. However if you set your goals using positive language, something like "I lose twenty pounds in weight and I constantly remain within two pounds of my target weight," is actively using both types of motivation.

So what has happened here to make such a difference? Well you have used away from motivation to start with. "I lose twenty pounds in weight" is moving away from where you are now. But then we activate our towards motivation. Saying "and I constantly remain within two pounds of my target weight" is a goal that you must move towards to achieve.

Likewise, our goal to be debt free would work much more effectively if we used the same techniques and language. Rather than saying "I will pay off my debts" we could say, "I am debt free and I have £500 untouched in a bank account." This ensures that we are moving away from the debt and towards the saving.

Believe You Can

Both of these goals means that we move up the mountain to get away from what we don't want, in this case debt and excess weight. However, when we are at the spot where we usually think about setting up camp ("at least I"), we then start climbing again to reach our next peak. And here is the most positive thing about it all. Because of the effort we have put in and the sense of achievement we feel once we are close to our goal at the peak, we are more likely to continue climbing because now we know what new success feels like. This is in sharp contrast to our usual feelings of failure caused by going back to base camp.

So how do we stay motivated enough to keep climbing?

Good question, and one that has baffled climbers since time immemorial. I guess there are many ways to remain motivated that even I have not heard of yet. However, here are a few of the techniques that I personally utilise to maintain my motivation to keep climbing.

Focus on your positive achievements instead of your negative results.

Easier said than done I know. But whatever it is that is tempting you to feel negative there WILL be something in the situation that merits celebration. Sometimes you might have to dig very deep to find a positive among all of your negative fallout but it will be there. Given the opportunity we could all sit down and play what the Monty Python team called the "Four Yorkshire Men" sketch. Man one: "I have had a bad day." Man two "You have had a bad day, you should have had my day," and so it goes on. Everyone trying to out do each other about their stinking day. However, it is just as easy to relate the positive things about your day as long as you are relating them to someone who gives a damn. (See next tip.) If all else fails relate them to yourself in the form of your achievements list. Write down your achievements, find a convenient mirror, and brag about them. There are enough outboards out there who will find something negative in situations. Be different. To coin a phrase my good friend Russell gave to me: *There are enough people out there who*

Believe You Can

tell it like it is. What we need are more people who tell it like it could be.

Remember the law of association

The law of association states that you will become a reflection of the people you are surrounded by. It is a fact that, given time, the actions, decisions and choices of those people you associate with will become your own. So surround yourself with positive people.

This might be a difficult exercise. If you are just starting out on your journey of personal development and releasing the magnificence that is you, there will be people whom you have associated with to this point who no longer fit into your vision of the future. These people (usually "for your own good") will attempt to hold you back. Their reasons, although difficult to comprehend, may well be purely honourable. The people you are associating with right now will have a desire to stay connected to you. Your newfound drive and enthusiasm could be perceived as a threat to your relationship with them. When you make a decision to attempt something with an element of risk involved they will make every effort to persuade you not to rock your boat. You know the type - "If it aint broke don't fix it." and other such motivational phrases. You will discover that these people, though they might THINK that they have your best interests at heart, are really holding you back because of their own fears. If you don't grow apart from these people naturally you may find that you have to let them go physically by making a conscious decision that they no longer fit into your future plans.

It will take time, effort and a considerable amount of courage to disassociate yourself from those people who, up until now, have seen you as an important part of their life. And whom you too could have seen as an equally important part of your life. It will be a difficult transition for you but one that you ***absolutely must*** take. Don't feel too bad about letting them go. Like water they will soon find their own level. They will become attached to others and others to them. In time you will be referred to as someone who "used to be a good laugh but now takes life too seriously."

Believe You Can

Once you have cleared the outboards from your address book you will find the spaces being taken by the people you want to be surrounded by. Your social circle will change completely. This is the time for you to decide who you want to associate with. And my guess is that you will want to associate with people who share your positive attitude and quest for success, or even people who have already achieved whatever it is that you are working towards. It's a fact that when I changed my attitude to life and began to emulate some of the people I used to envy, those people soon became a part of my peer group. If they didn't join naturally I went looking for them. You see I am a firm believer that I will become a reflection of the people I choose to surround myself with. To that end I am surrounding myself with people whom I admire, who I can help and who can help me. Most important of all though, by people who will not stand for my inadequacies.

One footnote here. I occasionally revisit some of my old watering holes, the gathering places of my old outboard friends. I still have conversations with them and some of them are still considered as friends. But I am aware that I have moved on considerably from where I was. Conversation is difficult because I am stimulated by more these days. I am also aware though that my old outboard associates are happy with who they are and what they are and that they have little or no interest in listening to me going on about "tree hugging woo woo stuff." I am regarded as someone who "just got lucky!" My re-visits are becoming less frequent and shorter.

Use positive self-talk:
We have mentioned positive self-talk previously in this book but it is such an important element of our success mentality that it won't hurt to mention it again. When was the last time you said something to yourself that would offend you if someone else said it to you? Probably on a daily basis if you are human. Imagine this: I take a negative phrase that you constantly use when you are speaking to yourself and I ask a group of strangers to repeat it to you constantly for a few hours. How do you think you would feel at the end of the exercise? Not good I bet? Well it is worth remembering that when

71

you speak to yourself in a negative way (or in a positive way for that matter) you are listening to yourself constantly. And it's no good saying, "I know I'm only joking." Consciously you might think so but unconsciously you are taking yourself seriously. Why not make a decision to never speak to yourself disrespectfully again, to always use positive statements when describing your actions and achievements. Again, like many other things in this book, I am asking you to change a habit of a lifetime so I don't expect you to change completely overnight. But you can start right now by changing a few simple phrases that you might use regularly.

Instead of saying:

"If" say "When?"

"I can't" say "How can I?"

"I will try" say "I will."

"I have to" say "I choose to."

"You stupid *%@*!" say "That's not like me."

Use congratulatory statements whenever you achieve something, no matter how small the achievement might be. A simple "Well done me." said with feeling can be the difference between a good session in the gym and an "I'm knackered!" It will soon become second nature to talk yourself up instead of running yourself down.

Never say anything to yourself that would offend you if someone else said it to you

Have a reason in the form of a vision:

I have lost count of how many times I have been asked the question "Why?" Why am I doing what I am doing? Why do I spend time away from my family and my home? And most of the time the person asking the question is *Me!* Any doubts I might have that I am doing whatever is right for myself and for those around me are dispelled by looking at my (our) vision. This is our reason in the form of pictures and words for doing what we are doing, for working so hard and for taking the risks that we take. We have a 'why' that is so strong that sometimes it even cancels out the need for a 'how.

Sara and I have a written Major Definite Purpose (see goal setting later) that explains exactly what it is we are working for, what it looks like, and includes when and how we will get there. Personally I have a number of pictures that I use in my vision of our future. These pictures might be of things or of places. The most important one though, and incidentally the one I look at most often, is a picture of Sara herself. It doesn't really matter what we have or where we are in the future as long as we have it, or are there, together. We just believe that we deserve some of the nice things (nice in our opinion) to enjoy our future with. So we work towards our vision together.

How to set and achieve personal and professional goals

Why should we bother to set goals?

Outboard motor's thoughts:

"I don't bother setting goals, whatever goal setting is. What's the point? If it was just about wishing what I wanted and setting a goal to get it, do you think I would be dragging myself out of bed every morning to go to this dead end job just so that I can pay my mortgage and a few bills?

And another thing, if all we had to do to be successful was to set goals do you think that c**p team I support would be languishing at the bottom of the league every year? Of course they b*'*"*y wouldn't! They would just set a goal to win and *we* could celebrate a trophy for once.

No mate, it's not about goal setting it's about *luck.* Luck is the only thing that is going to get me what I want. And I was born *unlucky* so it doesn't matter how many goals I set to get out of this miserable life I'm stuck here. And the sooner we all accept that the sooner we can get on with making it as painless as we can."

Typical conversation between me (positive person) and our outboard friend:

"Do you set goals?"

"I've just told you I don't set goals. Do you people never listen?"

"OK, sorry. But let me ask you a question, do you own a house?"

"Yes, what business is that of yours?"

"Are you still paying your mortgage?"

"Yes, what business is that of yours?"

Believe You Can

"When will your mortgage be fully paid off?"

*"Another fifteen b****y years. It's a millstone around my neck."*

"How do you pay your mortgage?"

"What is this, who wants to be a millionaire or something, I pay it off monthly same as everyone else."

"And do you know when you will have completed your goal of paying for your house?"

"Another eight years. Oy, don't you try dragging me in to your tree hugging stuff by saying I have a goal to own my own house!"

"But don't you see, by deciding you want to own a house and deciding when you can finally do that and then taking monthly steps to achieve house ownership that is indeed goal setting."

"Well spin me round and lock me in a phone box, you've got me on that one. But that was an accident. I'm ready for you now!"

"OK. Have you booked your holiday for next year yet?"

"Certainly have. Ten months and counting. Can't wait to get away from this place for two weeks."

"Have you paid for that yet?"

"Of course not. If I could afford to pay for it now I would go now."

"So you have booked a holiday that you can't afford to pay for right now. But you know you will have the money when the balance is due, isn't that goal setting too?"

"Doh!!"

Author's thoughts:

As we have just discovered with our outboard friend everyone, in some form or other, sets goals in their lives. Now if we could only get them doing it consciously we could create a tidal wave of success. Our friend, as usual, chose a very negative way of looking at life. But then our friend is an outboard motor and as we know they are not given to looking for reasons to be successful. They are though very good at finding reasons why they are not more successful. On this occasion it's the lack of luck. I have a challenge with the use of the word luck. In my definition, luck means *Labour Using Chosen Knowledge.* If this is true then purely accepting the definition will eliminate luck from the equation.

All successful people (no matter what your definition of success might be) are goal-oriented people. They know what they want and why they want it. More importantly though, they are prepared to focus on achieving their goals. They will work towards achieving them constantly until they are achieved. It was put fantastically well by one of my favourite authors, Earl Nightingale, when he said "You become what you think about most of the time." Successful people are consistently thinking about the positive things they do want to achieve. They know the requirements for setting and achieving their goals. Those requirements are:

Decide what it is that you want

Decide the price you must pay

Decide to start paying right now

They know that:

"To achieve something you have never achieved you must become someone you have never been."

In the opening chapter of this book I said that everyone had the power to close their eyes and dream. The challenge was that most people, when they open their eyes, see themselves as being back in the real world. They think that they are stuck with who they are and where they are. I hope you are beginning to realise by now that this is not the case. Anyone can change who he or she is or where he or she is simply by thinking differently. If it is true (and of course I believe it is) that there are absolutely no limits to what you can do, close your eyes and imagine that there can be no limits to what you can achieve.

Tapping into unused potential.

We have within us right now more potential than we could ever use in this lifetime. It is widely accepted though that we will only ever tap into about five percent of that potential. If that is the case then we must also be limiting ourselves to only ever enjoying five percent of the potential rewards and enjoyment that could be available to us. Setting positive goals for our future success and happiness will ensure that we use at least a little more of our potential by tapping into some of that hitherto unused potential.

When you think about it goal setting isn't that hard. In fact you are probably reading this book using some sort of goal setting techniques. My guess is that you haven't read it from cover to cover, not by accident anyway. You might have broken it down into chapters or time bound segments. You might even be reading it on your journey to work. (If you drive to work don't worry, the audio programme will be out soon.) I certainly wrote it using goal setting. Surprisingly enough I never sat down and wrote it in one go. I have written it one hour at a time or one thousand words at a time. When I started it I knew within a few pages how long it would be and how many chapters would be included. Whether you realise it or not you will also be using some sort of goal setting techniques in your everyday life. If you have a mortgage for instance, that could be one of the largest and longest term goals you will ever set. So if goal setting is so simple and something we do almost automatically, why do so few people have clear, specific, time bound and written goals?

Believe You Can

In my mind there are four main reasons why people don't have written and specific goals:

1. They don't know how to set written and specific goals

2. They don't understand the importance of setting goals

3. They fear ridicule or rejection of others

4. They fear failure

Four reasons why people don't have written and specific goals:

1.They don't know how to set written and specific goals.
I, and I guess most of you, spent over 1000 hours in education in my formative years. Throughout those years I cannot recall ever spending **one hour** being taught how to set goals. (Although I do recall being told on many occasions what I would not be able to do.) Some people think they have goals when in fact all they have are a series of wishes. Not a problem here, wishing is good. Most of the things we use on a day-to-day basis started off as either a wish or a dream. The challenge for most people is that they don't have a clue how to turn their wishes or dreams into goals and therefore into achievements. There is a definite difference between wishes and goals:

A wish is something you wish you could have or you wish would happen.

A goal is specific and can be described to others. It will have a time frame and you will know when you have achieved it.

Too many people think that the quaint little custom we have of setting New Year resolutions is goal setting. Most people who insist on setting New Year resolutions know the significance of the 14th of January or a similar such date. This is the date when enthusiasm starts to fade and they find themselves slipping back into their old ways. The truth is that they are not their old ways they are simply the same ways. They never really changed. The challenge with using this method for goal setting is that there are some major ingredients for successful goal setting missing. *Desire* and *commitment* are just two of those ingredients. A strong enough *why* is also usually conspicuous in its absence. Let's be honest here. After a period of sustained eating and drinking, such as the Christmas and New Year period, anyone could be slightly successful with a resolution to drink and eat less. Apart from anything else you have probably spent up after Christmas and New Year anyway. So staying in for a few weeks isn't really a challenge, not when you can't afford to go out anyway!

Goal setting is a skill and like any skill it must be practiced. The more you practice though the better you get, and the better you get the more goals you want to set for yourself. Starting small on a daily goal and working your way up to the great big, fat, juicy, audacious, long-term and lifetime goal is highly recommended. This is not a book on goal setting, it is a book on how to become the very best you can be. We will not be spending the rest of the book going through exactly how to set goals, we will just be introducing you to the concept and rules of setting goals. Although you will have a much greater understanding of the process, you will probably need a little more help to set your long-term goals. With that in mind (purely promotional bit coming up here!) might I suggest that you contact me to obtain a copy of my goal setting process "Live Life on Purpose." This is an audio programme with a workbook designed to take you through the process of setting goals from a simple (or magnificent) dream, right through to designing your *Major Definite Purpose.* Your MDP is the one goal that when you have achieved it will have the greatest positive impact on all of the other goals you might set yourself.

2. They don't understand the importance of setting goals.
If, as was the case with me, you are brought up in an environment where goal setting was never discussed. Where you never learned about it at school or it was never discussed around the dinner table.

Believe You Can

Perhaps you never associated, or indeed associate now, with people who set and achieve goals on a regular basis. If this is the case with you, it is a done deal that you will grow into the adult you become, not knowing that goal setting is the one skill that when you have developed it, will have the greatest positive impact on your future.

My guess is that you wouldn't go to a new town or city looking for a specific street or building without using a map first. The same would apply if you had a dream to build your own house. You would probably go through a series of exercises that would involve:

- Having a dream of what your house will look like when it is completed
- Deciding when and where your dream property will be completed
- Deciding on your budget and setting about obtaining the funds
- Having an architect draw up your plans
- Start digging and developing the foundations
- Start to build your house on to the foundations
- Have the builders check the plans every step of the way to ensure that what they are building is an exact replica of your dream
- Be willing to change if you hit an obstacle or have a better idea
- Celebrate your success when your magnificent dream is achieved

Doesn't it make sense that if you are prepared to go through that whole process to have somewhere nice to live, then it is just as important to go through the process to have a life to live in your nice place? Whether it is designing and building a house or designing and building your life, having clear written specific plans will ensure that you will build your house or your life by design and not by default.

Believe You Can

Writing down our goals also serves to activate a small part of our brain known as the reticular cortex. This, I understand, is a small appendage that takes up a small percentage of your brain.

Its job is to tune you into, or out of, things that you want to notice or not, whatever the case may be. It acts like a receptionist in your brain. Let's assume a travelling salesperson has cold called your office to see you. Your receptionist will decide (perhaps) whether it would be a good idea for you to meet them or not. If yes, they will let the person through and you will notice them. If no, they will not allow you to notice the presence of the salesperson.

Your reticular cortex acts in the same way. If you live, or know someone who lives, very close to an airport, the chances are that you think you no longer hear the planes taking off and landing. In truth you do hear them, you just don't notice them anymore. But people visiting you will wonder how on earth you live through this terrible noise. That is the work of your reticular cortex. Likewise, perhaps you have been recommended a book to read that you have never heard of before. The person recommending the book might say something like "I can't believe you haven't read it or at least seen it, it has been out for ages and is in the top ten list." You of course have never noticed it because up until now you have never had a reason to notice it. However, *every* bookshop or newsagents you pass from now on has it in their window. You might even start to notice that it is being advertised as a best seller in the newspaper or magazine that you read regularly. And when your weekly magazine is delivered at the weekend, guess which book is featured in its own two page article? The truth is that it has been displayed in the shop windows and advertised in the newspaper for weeks, you just haven't had a reason to notice it until now. But when your receptionist was told that you needed to notice it they stated to allow it through to your conscious mind.

The same will happen when you start to write down your goals. Writing them down will tell your reticular cortex (receptionist) that you need to start to notice things or people that will help you to achieve your goal. Those people or things have always been available to you, it's just that you didn't have a need to notice them … until now!

3. They fear ridicule or rejection from others.
Some people don't set goals because they fear what other people will think of them or say about them. Perhaps their peers will find their goal setting strange? Perhaps they will think that we now see ourselves as being "above our station." In reality, if your peers ridicule your goals it will be for a couple of reasons already covered in this book when we spoke of the law of association. Your peers or friends will fear your success because it might either take you away from them thus leaving them feeling rejected, or it could appear to show them up as underachievers themselves. Either way we must avoid this ridicule at all costs. And there is one sure fire way to stop other people ridiculing our goals. *Don't tell them!*

 It was put beautifully by Brian Tracy when he said on this subject, *"What they don't know can't hurt you."*

There are two people who you should share your goals with. Firstly, you should share them with someone who has an interest in your achievement of your goal(s). For instance if your goal is to become the best you can be at your career then your manager or someone similar will want to help you. After all, your success will reflect positively on them as well. If you want to run a marathon or achieve something equally as fantastic physically, then you should share your goals with your partner. Most physical goals like this will require a certain amount of your time and energy. If you are constantly fighting against someone else who requires that time and energy you are destined to underachieve. And (very important this one) you should also inform your partner if your goal is to move to a house with five bedrooms or bigger property.

You should also share your goals with someone like me who doesn't know or care what your goals are but we will do whatever we can to help you to achieve them. There are loads of us about who are willing to help. People who, because they have their own big fat juicy goals, have no fear of my success make up most of my social and business circle. In fact these people see it as complimentary to their own success to see me achieve my goals.

You won't have to look too far to find these people either. When you start living by the law of association they will find you. You might even receive an invitation to join a mastermind group of some sort. This is not a group of people with 'mini mes' sat on their shoulder, with a goal to take over the whole world and turn it into a gold mine. All we want to do is to share our thoughts and positive energy with other like-minded people who would like to do the same. People in your mastermind group will love and respect you enough to not tolerate your inadequacies. They will know what you are capable of achieving and will not allow you to get away with anything less. At the same time, they will expect the same support from you. Becoming a part of a mastermind group could well be the most positive thing you do to enhance your future success. If you do not receive an invitation to a mastermind group why not set up your own? Invite five or six people who you admire and trust. Arrange a meeting with them somewhere central to you all and decide what you want to achieve for yourself, for each other, and as a group. Set up a few rules of commitment and away you go.

4. They fear failure.
Setting a goal to achieve something absolutely fantastic and life changing, and then not achieving it, can be the most debilitating experience of anyone's life. This could happen for a number of reasons. Perhaps the goal was far too big to be achieved in the short time period allowed. Or the goal was not one that excited someone enough. Worst of all is when a goal is set using all of the tools and techniques correctly but not actually believing that you are worthy or capable of achieving it. Whatever the reason, *failure* to achieve a goal can be devastating. I have learned throughout the past few years that there is no such thing as failure, just differing levels of success.

Believe You Can

Dave Scott is arguably the finest Ironman triathlete who ever raced the distance. (For those philistines among you who don't know what an Ironman triathlon is, it is a race where you cover a 2.5 mile swim, followed by a 112 mile cycle, and finishing with a full 26.2 mile marathon run.) Until 1987 Dave Scott had never been beaten over the distance. His finishing time was usually around eight hours plus a few minutes. Personally, I have completed five of these races completing in times ranging from thirteen hours and forty-five minutes at my slowest to nine hours and thirty-six minutes at my best. When I was asked once how I would rate myself on a scale of one-to-ten if Dave Scott was a ten and a couch potato was at one, I thought I was being generous by putting myself at a five. I was shocked when I was told that I was more like a nine and a half. The only difference between Dave Scott and me was that he had covered the distance faster than I had. I learned that not only was I not a failure for 'only' doing nine hours and thirty-six minutes, but the couch potato was also doing what they wanted to do and they were probably very good at it. Certainly a much better couch potato than I could ever choose to be. So I learned that all three of us were successful, just to differing levels.

That is my round about way of saying that whatever goal you set for yourself, as long as you give it your best shot, you cannot fail. You might well come up with a result that you perhaps were not expecting, but you will come up with a result nevertheless. The following quote is (as with most of the quotes I use) not mine. But it does sum up this section beautifully.

Failure is a temporary situation.

Giving up makes it permanent.

Let's do a short exercise here. How many times have you tried to do something and, by your own definition, failed? What was the last thing you attempted and, by your own definition, failed at? My guess is that to get to a position where you think you failed you first had to be very successful. If you lost weight and then 'failed' by putting it all back on again (isn't that infuriating?) you did lose the weight in the first place so you were a success. The result you weren't expecting though was to put it back on again! It may have been a relationship that lasted for so long and then went belly up.

What was good about the relationship to that point that would indicate success before you achieved a result you weren't quite expecting? Maybe you are one of those people who have no challenges saving money until something comes along and you 'have' to spend it. This could indicate success with saving money but failure in retaining it. The truth is that in all of these examples you have been successful to a point. Just not as successful as those people who have taken your goal to the next level, which in these cases would be a happy life long relationship, permanent weight loss or consistent financial security.

To understand why this happens and how to take your present level of success to the next level, I suggest that you read the chapter on motivation again. You are successful at moving away from things and as soon as you achieve the same success at moving towards new things you will be achieving, and retaining, new things at will.

In the case of fear based reasons for not setting goals it might be worth repeating something we spoke of in our chapter on creating unshakeable self-confidence. Fear is just negative goal setting. We cannot fear the past just as we cannot regret the future. Therefore, if you have a fear it must be of the future, and the future hasn't happened yet so how on earth can you fear it. We can however fear repeating the past. And again, knowing that the future hasn't happened yet will enable us to make a decision not to do so. Making such a decision will enable us to think differently about how we approach the future. (If it is any consolation I had to read the last paragraph half a dozen times before it made complete sense!)

A few reasons why I believe we should have written and specific goals.

Believe You Can

If you have not set written, specific, time bound goals yet, you will probably find that your reason will fit loosely or firmly into one, or all, of the four reasons we have just discussed. You might even be able to add a few reasons of your own (let me know what they are please, I can use them in my next book). If this is the case you will probably also have your own reasons for not feeling completely fulfilled and, by your own definition, successful. That's fantastic because it means that you can now take full responsibility for your present position and make some serious decisions as to how you would like to move forward.

Let's just talk about personal responsibility for a while here. A sign of real maturity is when you realise that the cavalry isn't coming. The only person who can decide where you are going and how you can become, by your own definition, more successful, is you. I have a firm belief that we are who we are and where we are because of the person we have been, the beliefs we have had, and the actions we have taken up to this point. If you can buy into that then you can get really excited because where you go from here will be as a result of the person you become, the beliefs you adopt, and the actions you take from this point. Let me underline something here. Who you are is not **your fault**. Who you are is **your responsibility**. There is no blame when responsibility is present. The past should be used as a learning process, not as a tool to hold us back.

It doesn't matter where you have been.
All that really matters is where you are going.

So now we have got that straight let's stop blaming the past, including Mum and Dad and your least favourite teacher, and let's get on with creating our future. If you want things around you to change then you must change. If you want life to be different then you must be different. Are you getting the picture yet? I hope so. But just in case, here are a couple more little gems to help you. It has been said that the most important twenty letters in creating your own future are:

Believe You Can

"If it is to be it is up to me."

And finally, as good old Confucius himself said:

"A journey of a thousand miles begins with one small step."

Here are four reasons why I think it is important to set clearly defined, written and time bound goals:

1. It raises your self-esteem.

In my audio programme "Believe and Achieve" (*www.clivegott.com/beliveandachieve*) I describe the cycle of self-actualisation and how it works using the law of cause and effect. It works on the principle that our beliefs determine our expectations, which in turn will affect our attitude. Our attitude will influence our actions, which then help to determine our results. The upshot is that the results we are getting in our lives have a massive affect on our self-esteem. The whole cycle however revolves around the goals we set for ourselves.

It works like this. Let's stick with the weight loss thing again. If we set a goal to lose one kilogram in weight (2.2 pounds for us oldies) in two weeks, our belief will probably be fairly strong that we can do it. With such a strong belief we can expect to be successful. Having such positive expectations about our weight loss will determine that we have a positive attitude towards our task, and in turn will determine the actions that we take. In this case it will probably determine that we eat a little less and exercise a couple of times over the designated two-week period. Our actions will no doubt have the positive result of us losing the designated weight. Having achieved our weight loss, our self-esteem will probably, and justifiably, be higher than when we started. As a result, we will no doubt believe that if we can do it once we can do it again, and we will decide to lose another two kilograms over the next two weeks. The end result will be that because of our constant rise in self-esteem as a result of our continued weight loss, we will eventually reach the weight that we are happy to maintain in future. However, none of this would have happened if we had not initially set a small, specific and achievable goal to lose just two kilograms in two weeks. Simple really isn't it?

We can achieve exactly the same results in our relationships, our careers or our financial goals. Working a little bit at a time will raise our self-esteem a little bit at a time until one day **boom** you are up there flying with the Eagles and you didn't even realise how hard you were working to get there. There is a beautiful quote from a book I once read that says:

> *People are like butterflies.*
> *They think that they cannot fly….*
> *And then one day….*

And so it happens. People will say things like "Wow you look terrific, what did you do?" Or "I have never seen you so happy, what happened to you?" And all you will be able to say in return is "Thanks for noticing. All I did really was to raise my self-esteem by firstly believing in myself and in my ability to set and achieve small goals. My higher self-esteem then developed into greater self-belief, which helped me to set bigger and more challenging goals for myself. Achieving my goals and the subsequent goals I set for myself following my success, resulted in the confident, happy and, by my own definition, successful person that you see before you right now." Well OK you might not come out with all of that tree hugger clap trap, but you will be confident enough to just say "Thank you, I appreciate the compliment."

Taking charge of your own destiny by deciding exactly what it is that you want and then taking the relevant steps to achieve it will, without a shadow of a doubt, raise your self-esteem and self-worth through the roof.

2. It increases personal motivation.
Why do motivated people look forward to getting up in the morning? Why do they not have to 'drag' themselves to work like so many of

our outboard friends? Why do athletes put themselves through so much pain and pressure to achieve their goals? Why do I spend a great deal of my time away from my family and the home that we have worked so hard to put together? Why? Because we know why, that's why! Because we are motivated by what the results of our actions will bring. Put simply, having clearly defined, specific, measurable and achievable goals, gives meaning and purpose to whatever it is you are working towards. As we have already said in an earlier chapter (don't you love the way it all just flows? I didn't just throw this book together you know!), having a strong enough "why" will make any "how" possible. When you have a series of specific written goals you will find that you are never bored. Time becomes a currency and sleep becomes a necessary inconvenience. A short footnote here. Motivation is not something that will turn up eventually if you wait long enough.   Too many people use expressions like "I will start an exercise programme when I get the motivation."   Or "I will start the ironing, proposal writing or whatever the task is when I get motivated." ***WRONG!!!!*** Waiting for motivation to come is a sure fire way of never getting started. The truth is that motivation will come ***when*** you get started.

Motion creates emotion!

That's why having clearly defined goals with definite completion and start dates will ensure that you remain constantly motivated throughout the process.

Having clearly defined, written goals will also dispense with any "I'll just wait until" statements. You know how it works on this one. You want to start an exercise programme or a college course or even go for a new career but you have developed the skill of putting it off "just until!" I will start just as soon as:

The kids get back to school
(Usually associated with further education)
The new gym opens down the road
(Usually associated with starting to exercise)

I have paid off this credit card balance
(Usually associated with starting to save)
We have finished all of the food left over from Christmas (usually associated with New Year resolutions concerning diets)

I am certain that if I asked you to, you could send me a list of the reasons (excuses/ fears) you have been using to put off whatever it is you want to start. Having clearly defined, time bound goals will ensure that these excuses remain just that, excuses. *But For other people* and not for you. Because you will not only have a goal to achieve you will have a great big "why" and a clarified time frame for your success.

3. It 'appears ' to give you more time.

Time management's a fallacy. You cannot manage time. It is not your time to manage. Time is one of life's great levellers. We all have the same regardless of education or wealth. Sixty seconds, sixty minutes, twenty four hours, seven days, fifty two weeks and, on this earth anyway, one lifetime. *It is not your time, it is the time you have.* I have often wondered where reputedly busy managing directors and the like find three days to go on a time management programme! Imagine this. You are going to work on a Monday morning. You have the usual jobs to do and tasks to complete during the coming week, which under normal circumstances would put you under a certain amount of pressure to manage your time during the week. This week is a little different however, because at the end of this week you are out of here. Off on your holidays. The trip you have saved up an entire year for. If you are anything like me you will want everything tidied up before you leave so that you don't have to come back to any unfinished work or odd jobs. In short, you want to have a fantastic pressure free holiday and return to hit the ground running, ready to conquer the business world. How much work do you get done this week? My guess is all of it, and more besides. That is because this week you have prioritised more than usual. Nothing must get in the way of you enjoying your holiday. So where did the time come from to get everything done this particular week? There is not a decree of success that says you are

Believe You Can

entitled to an extra day if you are going on holiday. The time came from your efficient prioritising that's where. When you have a definitive reason to get everything done by a specific time it is amazing where you find the time to do it all. As I have said before in this book and I will no doubt say it again, when there is a strong enough "why" the "how" will take care of itself. Here is my question to you. Why not go on holiday every Friday? The only difference is that you will be coming back every Monday. But how much extra work will you get done with that attitude?

So how can we use goal setting to, apparently, give us more time? Well if you are a typical adult you probably sleep something like eight hours a day. And let's say you work somewhere around fifty hours a week. (You might work between forty and sixty; you do your own maths.) If this is the case you still have around *sixty-two hours a week* when you are neither sleeping nor working. When I discovered this in 1999 (reference "The Strangest Secret" by Earl Nightingale) I was blown away and immediately set about finding out what I did with my fifty-two hours a week. (I work about sixty hours a week.) I am not proud to say that a great deal of it was spent watching inane drivel on the TV. I would watch anything and everything. I would watch a programme of choice that perhaps lasted an hour. Then, while I was waiting for my next programme of choice, which probably didn't start for another hour, I would spend time flicking through the channels watching snippets of programmes for an hour to kill the time. By my own conservative estimates I could watch anything up to four hours a night and twelve hours over a weekend of any number of programmes designed to dumb my senses and encourage me to adopt an exercise routine designed for a two-toed sloth. That's somewhere in the region of *thirty-two hours a week* watching television. Now that can't be healthy can it?

Meanwhile, there were lots of small jobs that needed doing around the house and in the business that I just never seemed to have the time to do. Hmmmmm? Do you recognise anyone here? SO here is what I did. As well as the long-term goals I had already started to set myself at that time in my life, I took a conscious decision to utilise

Believe You Can

my time more productively by setting a series of small goals around the house and business. Goals (tasks or pain in the a*** jobs to our outboard friends) that would take anything from a few minutes to a few hours to complete, but that would make a significant difference to my life. So now **EVERY** Sunday afternoon I finish whatever I am doing in my office (I do about three hours in my office every Sunday afternoon) by completing my productive week list for the coming week. By the way, if I am due to travel abroad for a week I will do the list for two weeks. The list always looks the same. It is on one sheet of A4 paper only so that no goals are hidden on another sheet. There are seldom more than twenty goals on the list either.

My intention is to achieve as many of the goals as I can in the week or two weeks, and more than twenty would perhaps take too much of my focus off other things. I give my list the same title every time:

W/beginning (date) I will have had a productive week if I have:

I then list up to twenty things that, when I have achieved them, will ensure that I have had a productive week. The first two are always the same and are business related. They are:

Attended all of my appointments
Earned at least eight points

There then follows a list that can include such things as:

Had a haircut
Been to see my Mum
Been to the gym at least three times
Walked my dog four miles
Cleared out the drawers in my office
Booked the car in for a service
Called (whoever I need to call)
Written 6000 words for my book
Booked flight for next month
Mended the lock on the back gate

93

Cut the lawn, front and back

And so on. It is absolutely amazing how much you can get done in just seven days when you actually have a list of what you could do to ensure a productive week. One footnote here. When I have completed a goal I **never** cross it off. Crossing something out reminds me of doing something wrong at school. When I have been successful in achieving something I highlight it using a yellow or orange highlighter pen. This way at the end of the week I can look at my list on my office wall and see nothing but a block of colour. And that, to me at least, signifies a successful week as far as "doing stuff" is concerned.

Another way to look at the "wish I could but I don't have time" syndrome is to look at what you **could** do if you broke your fifty-two or sixty-two hours a week down into what you would do if you could, and how much time each one would take. For instance, if you work fifty hours a week that leaves sixty-two hours when you are not working or sleeping

- *Three hours a week at the gym leaves fifty-nine hours*
- *Half an hour a day reading leaves fifty-five and a half hours*
- *Travelling to work (two hours daily) leaves forty-five and a half hours*
- *Eating and preparing food (two hours daily) leaves thirty-five and a half hours*
- *Ten hours a week socialising with friends, at the game, pub etc. leaves twenty-five and a half hours*
- *Ten hours a week watching TV leaves fifteen and a half hours*

And so it goes on. I know this all looks a little like utopia, "What about the kids and so on?" but you can put what you want in the spaces. The fact is that we have all got the same time on our hands. People who set goals on a regular basis just *'appear'* to have more time because they use it wisely. They use their time how they choose to use it. So next time someone asks you if you have the time to do something or go somewhere that you don't want to do or go to, you don't have to use the excuse "Sorry I don't have time." Now you can tell the truth. "I do have the time, but I choose to use it for something else."

4. It stops you living a script.
I know some of you young uns reading this book won't remember this but it is not so long ago that people expected to have jobs for life. And many of those jobs were seen as hereditary. Where I come from in the North of England, coal mining was seen as a job for life as was working for the railways or at one of the breweries that are local to my hometown. Not only did the adult have a job for life but is was widely regarded that the children of the family (certainly the males) would follow their fathers into the industry. In many cases the son would follow his father into the same job, as he had followed his father into the job. There was little or no need for career advice in school because your future had been mapped out since the day you were born. For the most part those days are now gone. Now there is a much wider choice. Now we can actually write our own scripts for our future, we don't have to follow the one written for us and passed down through the years.

The same applies to social lives and the like. Look around you at your social circle. Are you spending time with the people you want to spend time with or has your social circle become a habit? Are they part of the script that has been written for you? I cringe when I hear young people described as "typical teenagers." For typical teenagers read instead "they are following the script written for them by someone else." In the worst possible scenario drug dealers or petty criminals could have written that script for them. Think about Oliver Twist, a simple story where one man, Fagin, had written the script for a group of small boys. With no other script to follow the boys were easy prey for the leader of the gang who duly turned them into pick pockets to satisfy his own ends.

Believe You Can

Similar situations are still around today only in this modern age the product is not the odd wallet that is stolen from the pocket of the gentry. Today's 'Fagins' are drug dealers or car thieves. These are the scriptwriters, and the wayward, 'bored' young people are their actors. People, young and old alike, need not follow any script written by someone else. All they need to do is write their own. They can be the Audey Murphy of their own lives. (For those among you who are going "Who?" Mr Murphy was an American war hero and winner of the Purple Heart who wrote, produced, directed and stared in a film about his life.)

Earl Nightingale talks about people who "follow the followers." These are people who just go along with the crowd in the forlorn hope that the crowd is going where they want to go. And it is not usually the case. If you want to follow someone, that's fine. If you know someone who is where you want to be or who has whatever it is you are working towards then by all means follow them, at least until you have the courage or knowledge to go your own way. But don't just go along with the crowd because you think they know where they are going because the chances are that they don't. You could end up so far behind in life that it actually looks like you are in front. Make sure that the person you are following is going where you want to go.

Deciding what it is you want to achieve and then creating an action plan to achieve it (goal setting) is a sure fire way to avoid any script that might have been written for you in the past. And by knowing exactly what it is you want or where you want to be it will make it easier for you to identify the people you should choose to follow.

A person without a goal is like a ship without a rudder.

So there you have it, those are the four major reasons why most people don't, and successful people do, set goals. My guess is that if you don't yet set your own goals, your reasons why not will have been covered at some point. And if you already do set your own goals you might now have a greater understanding of why you do and the benefits of doing so. It might be that you are like our outboard friend at the beginning of this chapter who previously thought goal setting was nonsense for tree huggers and an excuse used to explain away pure luck. Only to find that you too have been setting goals for yourself all along but without consciously knowing it. Now you are aware of it you can do it constructively can't you.

You would think that after all of that you are now ready to go and decide whatever it is you want, write it down and go ahead and get it. You would think so ... but no, not yet. There is one more subject for us to cover before I let you loose on designing your future. We have to discuss the rules of setting goals. Yes I know, you just want to get on with living your life on purpose and now I'm throwing a bunch of rules at you. Well I'm sorry but it has to be done. My one disclaimer here is that if you appreciate the four reasons why successful people set goals, and you follow these rules, ninety percent of you will achieve things in your life beyond your wildest dreams. Why only ninety percent? Because some of you will read through this book and then put it down and do absolutely nothing with it.

Which one are you going to be? Let's discuss some of the rules of goal setting.

The rules of goal setting.

Outboard's thoughts:

"See I told you it was all mumbo jumbo. If this goal setting thing is so good how come you have to go around setting rules for the whole thing. Surely this just underlines what I have been saying all along, that this success thing is OK for others but the rest of us still have to do whatever it is that you tell us to do. If this goal setting thing is everything you make it out to be why can't we just go ahead and set our goals willy nilly and as we like?"

Believe You Can

Author's thoughts:

Oh dear oh dear, we are feeling a little bitter today aren't we? Of course we need to have a few rules as far as setting our goals are concerned. Hopefully by the end of this chapter you will understand why. But for the moment let me explain it this way. If there were no rules to setting goals we would be destined to 'fail' at many of the goals we set, for a number of reasons. Perhaps we are setting a goal for someone else, which is a big no no. Maybe we set a goal but gave ourselves too short a time frame for its achievement; a sure sign that we would not be happy about attempting something again. It might even be that we set a goal so great and so time consuming that we completely ignore the rest of our lives and the people in it. That is one way to achieve whatever you want in one area of your life but lose everything in the other areas that need attention. So you see we have to consider other things and people if we want to achieve our goals and maintain a well-balanced life as well. So let's have a chat about the rules of goal setting.

Rule one: YOU and only YOU must believe it is possible.
The history of success is littered with examples of how people have challenged limiting beliefs and achieved the seemingly impossible. If I felt it relevant I could even use my own example here. (I obviously feel it relevant or I wouldn't be telling you eh?) I mean, who on earth believes anyone who weighs over twenty stone can go on to run a marathon in a little over three hours, and complete an Ironman triathlon in nine hours and thirty-six minutes. A feat like that is just not possible. It would be pertinent to tell you here that when I started to lose my weight all those years ago I wasn't altogether sure I could do it either, in fact the Ironman bit wasn't even a consideration. But I lost the weight and ran the marathon so why not do the Ironman thing. I have very much the same mentality now when it comes to life and business goals. My belief is that if I can do the Ironman thing I can do anything, as long as I have a strong enough "why." When I share my goals (I'm not too bothered who I share them with but you should be a little cautious as I explained in the last chapter) I am invariably asked by the outboards "How do

Believe You Can

you know you can do it. What makes you so special?" You can probably guess my answer. "I don't. But how do you know I can't?" And off we go following our own separate paths. Them believing I can't do it and me just getting on and doing it.

At this point, if I was like every other personal development speaker or author, I would tell you about Sir Roger Banister. He is the guy who, on Wednesday 6th May 1954 at an insignificant athletics meeting on a small running track in Oxford, became the first human being to run a measured mile in under four minutes. I would tell you how he was told prior to his attempt that his lungs would explode and his heart would come out on to the track. I would tell you how **he** believed though that it **was** possible for a human being to run that fast. I would then tell you that, with the help of two great friends and athletes, he went on to prove all of the experts wrong and he ran a mile in under four minutes. Three minutes, fifty-nine point nine seconds to be precise. I would also tell you that because of his achievement he changed the thinking of every other world class mile runner. I would tell you that because his belief was so great that he could achieve the 'impossible', he changed the face of athletics forever. I would go on to say that once he had achieved something that most others did not think was possible he removed any last doubt and negative belief that running a mile in under four minutes was possible. The result is that every metric mile race (or its modern equivalent) run in a major championship since then has been won in a time less than four minutes. If I was like everyone else I would tell you that, but I'm not like everyone else so I won't tell you one of the most famous stories of human achievement over negative beliefs. But if I did that is what I would have told you.

However, if I had told you the same old story, what would have been the conclusion? If it was always previously thought to be almost impossible for a human to run that fast and now all races are won in even faster times, what had changed. Initially it was not the training styles or the nutritional intake of the athletes. It was not that a revolutionary discovery in the design of equipment had been made. Neither was it a major improvement in track design. All that Sir

Roger Banister changed was *the belief* that it was possible to run so fast.

I'm not too sure why the outboards told Sir Roger that his goal was impossible. Perhaps they actually believed that it was impossible. Perhaps they thought it was possible but they wanted to do it first. Or perhaps they thought it was possible, but if he achieved it they would no longer have an excuse for not getting off their backsides and achieving the feat themselves. Whatever the reasons of the outboards that told him he couldn't do it were, those reasons were not congruent with his own beliefs. As a result he chose to ignore them and do it anyway. And we must do the same. I have no idea what your goals are but I do know that someone somewhere will have a brilliant and easily provable reason why it is not possible for you to achieve it/them. They could be right, as far as them achieving your goals are concerned. But they are not you. So if you believe that your goal is possible, that is all the belief you need. And one other thing, you don't even need to know how. If your belief that you "can" is strong enough, your "how" will take care of itself.

2. Your goals must be purely personal.

It is very easy to fall into the trap of setting goals for other people. Especially if, like me, you are a parent and you want *the very best* for your kids. That is all very well if what you think is the very best for them and what they think is the very best for them are the same things. And there by hangs a question. Like "How does Teflon stick to the pan?" or "Where is the next generation of seedless grapes coming from?" "What do you think is best for me Dad?" is one of those questions that are seldom going to be followed by an agreeable answer.

The same applies in the workplace between managers and employees or team members. The goals that you would set or have set in the past to achieve certain tasks or targets, may not work as well for other people in the same situation. Before we go on let's put something straight here. *Targets* are targets and *goals* are goals. A target is usually set by someone else and is invariably non-negotiable. Whereas a goal is personal, set by the individual or team for their own achievements, and based upon their own motivation or reasons why. An individual or team target set within the workplace will be set based on the requirements of the organisation. Likewise, a target set by a parent for their children will be set based upon the requirements of the oppressive regime that is parenting (Your children's speak for firm handed parenting).

Let's say that a sales team has been given a particular income target for the month, say £60,000. That is the target set by the management, and that target in itself is non-negotiable. How the team or individuals reach that target though is down to the personal goals they set. An individual who "doesn't do mornings" for instance is not likely to respond well to an imposed goal of making ten calls before breakfast. Likewise, a predominantly away from motivated individual is unlikely to see a need to panic much before the last quarter of the month. But then stand back and watch them go. If you leave a list of jobs for the kids to do before you get home the same applies. Don't expect any progress until the soap opera has finished or until they hear your car pull up on the drive. I learned all about this stuff when my baby (she's 19 right now but will always be

my baby) was studying for her final exams at college. She was probably sick of hearing me saying "You need to focus more" or "Don't you think you should be at home studying instead of going out and enjoying your formative years with friends?" All of this 'good' advice by the way was coming from a bloke whose only major qualification is a driving licence. And I am hanging on to that by the skin of my teeth. My advice was given with the best of intentions. But it was probably received at best, as intrusive. At worst it could have been perceived as bullying, or as me trying to make her achieve the things that I never managed to achieve. She did it her own way, passing several major examinations on the way and securing herself a place in the university of her choice. How she did it without following the steps that I thought it would be best for her to follow, I will never know. But she did. And it was all down to her setting her own goals based upon her own motivation and a strong enough "Why?" The situation will level itself out when she sets herself a goal to "get Dad to buy me a car!"

So you see goals are just about as personal as you can get. I have a positive habit of writing down a list of some of my major goals every morning in a small booklet. Two of those goals are for my wife and myself. I have her permission to write those goals down. I need her permission because she has to buy into the goals for them to be personalised by both of us. We both discussed the goals and we both agreed on just about every aspect of the end product (with the exception of the colour).

So there you have it, our goals must be purely personal. Our outboard might say, "How selfish is that?" And they would be correct. Setting personal goals is selfish. But as I have already explained, one of my major goals is to be together forever with my beautiful wife. A personal goal yes, but one that requires her agreement (I have it) and a considerable amount of input from her to make it happen.

3.   Your goals must be balanced.
If you took a decision to focus your entire efforts on becoming, by you're own standards, financially wealthy over the next five years or so, and if you decided to focus one hundred percent of your attention to that goal, to the exclusion of everything else around you, then, having made your choice, you did just that, you focused on your goal to become financially wealthy within five years, my guess is you would make it. However, I also think that you would be missing a great many things in your life that you could be enjoying had you either decided to go for a little less financial success or decided to take a little longer in achieving your success. Personally, I firmly believe that you can have just about anything you want in life, but you can't have everything you want in life. At least not all straight away anyway.

There are several schools of thought as to what are the different areas of our lives that we could / should focus on. I think Jack Black talks about eight areas and Zig Ziglar talks about seven. Personally I talk about six areas of your life that, if you pay an equal amount of attention to each, will ensure that you have as balanced a life as you possibly can. I believe those areas are:

- *Relationships*
- *Career*
- *Physical*
- *Personal / mental development*
- *Spiritual / community*
- *Financial*

Let's look a little closer at each area.

Relationships covers the people you live with and who directly influence your lives and the goals you choose to set and achieve. This area also covers the other relationships you are likely to have or encounter, the people you work with, and the relationships that make up your social life. Remember what we said about the law of association. Are you associating with the people you want to become? Take a look at your address book and if necessary give it a clean out. Remember you will become a reflection of your environment, and that includes the people you associate with.

Career. We spend something like one third of our lives at work. What will you say about your career when it is over? How do you feel when you set off to work in the morning, or whenever you choose to set off? Have you got to go to work or do you get to go to work? How clear are you about the career you would truly like to pursue and how you would really like to earn your living?

Physical. This is probably the area that gives the people I have come into contact with the least pleasure. "I need to lose weight" or "I would like to be fitter" are two of the most common expressions I hear. The challenge comes when I ask "Exactly how much weight?" or "What exactly does get fitter mean to you?" How would you rate yourself physically right now by your own standards, not in relation to whoever won the latest televised marathon in just over two hours.

Believe You Can

Personal development / Mental. This area is designed to make you think about your own development as an individual. My guess is that most of us would be unhappy about working for someone or an organisation who refused to put any of their profits into developing their people. But how much of your own income do you put into developing yourself. Most of the people I know spend more on maintaining their cars and houses than they do on maintaining their minds. As far as achieving your wildest dreams is concerned, developing yourself mentally is up with maintaining a regular intake of oxygen.

Spiritual / Community. What are you doing to ensure that when you leave this planet it is going to be a better place for you having been here? What are you giving back? Have you ever grumbled about there being a lack of facilities for your area or that there is nowhere for the kids to play? Do you moan about local politics or that fact that no one seems to care any more? If so what have you done about it? What could you do, with enthusiasm, which would improve your community? What are your spiritual goals (if you have them)? By the way, if you have no wish to improve yourself spiritually or to improve your community in any way, please don't beat yourself up about this section, but don't complain when things aren't exactly as you would like them to be either.

Financial. This section includes all aspects of your life financially. Your earnings, your spending and your savings included. How much do you have saved and how is it invested. How much do you have put aside for a rainy day? My wife and I decided that we would feel comfortable with our investment risks if we have three months worth of outgoings put aside. So before we started any investments we concentrated on this goal first. According to Brian Tracy, most households are only two month's salary payments away from eviction. That means that in a great many households, if the major income was stopped completely for any reason, and for two months or more, the people involved would be in danger of losing their home. How do you rate on this score? Will you have to work right up until retirement age, and if so will you be totally reliant on the state pension, if indeed there is a state pension. It is rumoured that as we stand today (28-04-04) we may well be the last generation, in the UK at least, guaranteed a state pension of any kind. Don't be one of those people who, by the time they reach seventy years or older are either dead or dead broke.

Those are the six areas that I see our lives dividing up into. Any other areas will fit loosely or firmly into one or all of those areas. In my goal setting programme "Live Life on Purpose" you will be guided through an exercise that will help you to discover exactly where you think you are right now in all of those six areas. In doing so you will discover the shape of the wheel on which you are journeying through your life at present. And how smooth your journey through life is right now. For now though, just look back through all six areas and give yourself a score between one and ten (one is low, ten is high) as to where you see yourself in each area right now. If you find yourself with a particularly low score in one area and an equally high score in another you might like to think about diverting a little of your attention from the high score (which is probably something you really enjoy doing) to the area with the lower score (which is probably the area you least like doing but that you know you *should* pay more attention to). As I said, if we could pay an equal amount of attention to each of these areas we would probably have a very smooth journey through life. But it doesn't work like that does it. We would love to spend more time with our families as well as pay full attention to our physical well-being and development. At the same time, we realise the need to maintain and advance our career so that we can sustain the financial side of life.

And we would just love to find the time to spend doing things for the community such as working at the local school, or with the kids in the youth club. And remember that we also have a goal to study for the MBA that we so desperately need to fulfil our disappointment at not achieving as much as we could have done at school. The challenge comes when we want to do something, but to do that something would mean that we could not do something else. That would result in our upsetting someone else who really wanted us to be there when they were doing the something else. So because you can't do a particular something, because you really want to do something else and at the same time you don't want to upset anyone, you end up doing everything but not very well. Or worse still you end up doing nothing and getting completely frustrated about the whole thing. We will talk about the time thing in a moment but for now let's talk about balance.

In the late 1980s I was at my physical peak. I was running marathons at will and I was fortunate enough to have the opportunity to travel to some wonderful places, taking part in some gruelling triathlon and marathon races. Between 1989 and 1995 I was fortunate enough to take part in races in places like Auckland New Zealand, Perth Australia, Las Vegas USA, Germany, France and Montreal Canada. I was having a wonderful time fulfilling my dreams and achieving all of my athletic and travel goals. However, I was completely neglecting my marriage and by late 1990 it was in ruins. My wife and I separated and eventually divorced. Me? I just carried on doing what I was doing. *That is what happens when you have goals that are completely unbalanced and incongruent with your desired lifestyle.* That was not an easy way to learn about having balance in your life. But it was nevertheless a lesson I took notice of. I still have goals now, some of them so audacious that I wouldn't dream of putting them in this book. The difference now though is that all of the goals that I have are complimentary to any other goals that I have. And I share them with those people around me who are important and whose help I need to bring them to fruition.

You can avoid, or at least lessen your chances of an unbalanced lifestyle, by paying attention to what it is that you want and the effect it will have on the people you would like to spend your life with. You will find yourself perhaps saying no to some goals even accepting someone else's goals as a means of spending time with loved ones. You might find yourself choosing to do more of some things and less of others. You could even find yourself saying yes to some things and no to others. Spending less time on your goals for

Believe You Can

your community may seem a little selfish to some observers, but if it means that you can spend more time with your family what does it matter what other people think? Deciding to run a marathon in three years' time instead of next year, will stretch the goal out a little but will mean that you don't have to spend so long every week out of the house away from your family. Deciding that this piece of c**p car will last another two years (at least) might mean that you don't look as good to the outside world as you would in a brand spanking new car. But it might mean that you could finally have the holiday you have always said you would like, or the new kitchen or house that is also on the goal list

And what about those budding sports stars of the future, some of which I have the absolute privilege to work with. If your goal is to become an international sports person but you don't want to stop going out with your mates, you are going to find that one or the other, or even both of them, suffer. Find a way around your dilemma or make a choice. Whether you are a budding sports star, a high flying business person, or simply looking for a happy and contented relationship, you will find that compromise and consideration for others will go a long way in helping you to achieve everything that you truly desire. It is not just another clever saying or quote. I honestly believe that *you can have anything you want but you can't have everything you want right now.*

4. Live for now.

> *Yesterday is history*
> *Tomorrow is a mystery*
> *Today is a gift*
> *That is why they call it the present.*

It's all very well having those great big hairy audacious goals plonked way out there on your time lines, five, ten or twenty years away. But what about today? I read a question somewhere once that asked *if you had three minutes to live, who would you call, what would you say and what are you waiting for?*

107

Believe You Can

I am a firm believer in having goals for the future. As I sit here today writing this chapter (it is the 27th April 2004), I have goals set as far away as August 2008 and if truth be known, well beyond that date too. But I also have goals for today, tomorrow, next week, next month and the rest of this year. I don't want to have my fiftieth birthday party on my own except for my close family and a young lady who looks remarkably like my daughter did all those years ago. I want to know who she is and what she has been up to for the last few years. I don't want to have a thriving and highly lucrative business but a bored and neglected family.

I once saw a television commercial for VW motor cars. It showed a driver taking the long way round for a relatively short journey because he or she just liked driving their car. The strap line at the end simply said "the pleasure is in the journey, not in arriving." I remember thinking what a fantastic statement that was, and a very effective way of putting it across as well. So by all means set your fantastic goals. Have a dream of living to over 100, of becoming fantastically wealthy by your own definition. Set your goals to run your marathon or to build your house. Lay down plans to travel the world and see the remaining wonders. Decide to reach the highest levels within your organisation. Have all of those goals and more besides. But keep one eye at least on the present. You are older now that you were when you started to read this chapter. That time will never be yours again, it is gone forever. On this occasion you chose to use your time well. Make sure that your future decisions are just as wise. If you want to watch a particular programme on TV and someone close to you would appreciate some of your time right now remember this - the programme will most likely be repeated, the chance to help a loved one or friend might not.

5. Set only positive goals.
I seem to recall that we discussed the power of away from and towards motivation in an earlier chapter, so you already know and understand the power of camping and climbing. But I did promise you a more in depth discussion about the perils of setting negative

goals. Campers, as you will recall, are very good at setting away from goals. These can sometimes be looked upon as negative goals.

- *"I don't want to be late."*
- *"I don't want to be unhappy any more."*
- *" I need to lose some weight."*
- *"I want to pay off my debts."*
- *"I don't want to work here any more."*
- *"I don't want to smoke any more."*

All of these goals, and the hundreds of others that you and I have voiced over the years, are negative goals. Do me a favour please, for the next thirty seconds don't think about the worst holiday you have ever had…………..

…………………. If you recall, I said *don't* think about the worst holiday you have ever had. Don't you listen? What were you thinking about as soon as you read that sentence? You see to not think about something, you have to think about it first so that you can stop thinking about it. Before you read that sentence you probably hadn't given a second thought to the worst holiday you have ever had, but now you mention it! Now I want you to think about your favourite meal …………

………… There, that's much better isn't it? You see the power of thought. "Don't think about your worst holiday" is a goal. A negative goal I admit but nevertheless a goal all the same. "Do think about your favourite meal" is also a goal. Only this time you were thinking about what you wanted to think about and not about what you didn't want to think about. Does that make sense? I hope so because I got lost somewhere there.

Setting a goal using words like "I don't want to be late" is a negative goal. The reason being that as soon as you have said it, even to yourself, you then have to start thinking about ways that you can achieve the goal you have just set yourself, which is to be late. Whereas setting a goal by using words like "I will be early," or if you want to be even more specific, "I will arrive before eight thirty tomorrow morning," is programming your mind to think of ways that you could achieve your goal.

Using negative language to set goals is a sure fire way to make sure you never achieve them. Let me ask you a question. If your goal is to "pay off my debts" what do you need to have before you can achieve your goal?

- *Money? No*
- *A plan? No*
- *Motivation to pay off your debts? No*
- *A job? No*

OK let me ask you another question. If your goal is "to lose some weight" what do you need to be before you can achieve your goal?

- *Motivated? No*
- *A member of a gym? No*
- *Know how much you weigh? No (well yes but not in this case)*

The answer to the first question is debts, and to the second overweight. Before you can achieve a goal to pay off your debts you have to be in debt. And before you can achieve a goal to lose weight you have to perceive yourself as being overweight.

Let's say that you are something like £2500 in debt. You set a goal to "pay off my debts." Every morning you say to yourself "I must pay off these debts." You spend all of your spare time thinking of ways to "pay off these debts." You even take a second job to help you to "pay off these debts." Then, after a lot of effort, you get your debt down to just £200. Your unconscious mind starts saying things to you like "If you don't run up some more debts soon I won't have any goals." And then you find yourself "having" to spend some money on something that last week you had never heard of but this week you need it just to survive. And so the journey back to 'normal'

110

Believe You Can

starts all over again. It is the same with the negative "I need to lose some weight" goal. That's why people have no problem whatsoever in losing weight. It is keeping the stuff off that is the challenge.

Why not set positive goals like "I weigh (however many kg) and I maintain that weight for the next five years." Or constantly, or however you want to word the last bit. How about, instead of "I must pay off my debts" you say or write something like "I am debt free and I have £1000 in the bank untouched."

The same applies to sports people or teams. A team who sets a goal to win will constantly be thinking of ways that they can win. The team who set a goal not to lose will constantly be thinking of ways that they might lose the game.

What about the sales person who doesn't want to be the worst performer for the year? A goal that states, "I don't want to be bottom of the performance table" will ensure that the individual will be thinking constantly about what it would take and feel like to be bottom of the team. The same goal worded positively, something like "I am the top performer" or "I am in the top three performers" will have them thinking about ways that they can achieve their positive goal. So when it comes to setting your goals, make sure you tell your unconscious mind what you *do* want and not what you *don't* want. Because whatever you think about is what you will get.

Now whatever you do ***don't start thinking about all of the people you could buy this book for as a birthday or Christmas gift.***

5.Your goals must be time phased. My great friend Tracie once told me that "you can't do everything at once, but you can do something at once." As I mentioned earlier, I am a great fan of plonking great big, fat, hairy, audacious goals out there on a time line, so that you can work towards them gradually and with respect for others. But it would be irresponsible of me to tell you that all you need is a goal, some unshakeable belief and a smattering of enthusiasm, and you can have anything and everything you want right now. That is not going to happen. But given time you can move closer to achieving any, and all, of the dreams and goals that you truly desire.

Time is the most flexible of all of the rules in goal setting. Having a time and date for the achievement for your goals and dreams is meant to help you to become focussed on the goal at the outset. However, staying focused on the goal rather than the time line, will go a long way to maintaining your enthusiasm for achieving your goals. It will also help when those little obstacles called challenges pop up from time to time. For example, if you board an aeroplane from London to Sydney, you will have been given a time that the pilot expects to arrive at the destination. If you hit bad weather, or any other obstacles along the way that delay the flight, you will still end up at your destination. The worst that will happen probably is that you might be late in arriving, but you **will** arrive. At no time in the journey will the pilot say to their co-pilot "let's go to New York instead." No matter what happens they will always remain focussed on their goal and pay less attention to the time line.   Another example might be running a marathon. If you train for a marathon and one week before the race you pull a muscle making it impossible to complete the race at that time, it only means that you cannot run that particular marathon. It does not mean that you can never run the race, you just can't run *that* race. Be flexible with your time lines and remember:

> *"You can't do everything at once*
> *but you can do something at once."*

So there we have it. Four reasons why people don't set goals, four reasons why successful people do set goals, and six rules for effective goal setting. You would think that it was all done now wouldn't you? Well it is … almost. We just need to clear up a few steps we should take to make us define our goals clearly and specifically. (You just know I'm going to use SMART somewhere here don't you?) And finally, how do we decide upon our *Major Definite Purpose* (MDP from now on)? So let's explore the steps to goal setting and then we can be on our way. It is not my intention to go too deeply into this section as it is covered in great depth in "Live Life on Purpose." But here is a simple explanation to get you started.

Step one
Know your dream. We all dream. You can close your eyes and dream right now. But as we have already said, most people open their eyes and discover that they are back in the real world again. So you can decide to be different. You can dream and eliminate the word "Why?" from the equation. Take five minutes to do this exercise. Even if you have done it previously do it again, it will serve to reinforce your dreams. Take some time out right now to write down some of your dreams on a piece of paper, or better still in your journal (you do have a journal don't you?). What is it that you have always thought, or even said out loud, that you have always wanted to have, be, do, see, create, or write? Where have you always wanted to visit? Who have you always said you wanted to meet? Do this exercise without the usual "But how?" limitations. Go mad for once. What would you give one hundred percent to achieving if you knew you were guaranteed to succeed? You might like to think about what you would like to achieve in all six of the areas of your life we discussed in the rule on your goals being balanced.

Step two
A goal is a dream with a date attached. You are now at the point where most people say "Right, where was I before I was so rudely interrupted by that tree hugger?" But you are different. You have made it this far through this book so you must have some staying power. And who knows, you might even have a much higher level of self-belief now as well? So we can go on to the next step, which is giving some of your dreams a date. Take a look down your dream list. Decide which dreams you would like to take to the next step. To keep your life in balance, once again you might like to decide on certain goals in all six areas of your life. These dreams need a date, or at least a loose time frame, to take them to the next step. Decide which dream(s) you would like to turn into goals and identify them

by putting a time or date next to them. It does not have to be too specific at this point. 2Y for two years or 6M for six months will suffice for now. You don't have to include all of your dreams either. You might decide to leave some of them until you have more confidence or time to turn them into goals. When you have completed this exercise do the following exercise:

Stand up and stretch your right arm out in front of you.

Bend your right arm at the elbow so that your right hand is on your left shoulder.

Pat yourself on your back profusely and say "Congratulations me." You have now put yourself in the minority of the world's population by writing down some of your goals.

Step three
Decide upon your ten most important goals. By most important I mean which ten goals, when you have achieved them, will have the greatest positive effect on your future success? Selecting these ten goals does not discount or undervalue any of the other goals you have decided to adopt. It just means that achieving these ten will have the greatest positive effect on all of the others.

Step four
Decide upon your most important three goals. Again, by most important I mean which three goals, when you have achieved them, will have the greatest positive effect on all of your other goals. These goals need to be written down in a little more detail. We need to put some action steps with time frames to these goals. What is the first step you need to take in achieving your goal? What next and so on. In a recent workshop I was delivering one of the delegates had decided that learning how to use PowerPoint on his computer was a top three goal for him. His first step was to buy a book on the subject. Other steps were to find a college programme or course, then enrol, and so on. His final step was to deliver a presentation, on a specific day, to a specific group, using his new skills with

PowerPoint. As a footnote he also wrote down the reaction he expected from his audience on completion of the presentation. **Powerful visualisation indeed.**

You should follow your action steps with a brief action plan, including approximate dates, as to how and when you intend to carry out your steps.

Step four
Deciding on your *Major Definite Purpose*.
This could well be the most difficult part of the exercise. You must now decide which **one** goal you will adopt as your MDP. Which goal, when you have achieved it, will have the greatest positive impact on all of your other goals and on your future success? When you have decided on your MDP it is absolutely essential that you write it down, with absolute clarity, in such a way that you can almost feel the success before you even start out on the journey to achieving it. And this is where our old friend S.M.A.R.T. comes in to the equation.

There are many people out there who will claim to have invented the S.M.A.R.T. formula. I am not one of them. I have met one of them though. Funnily enough, the same person also claimed to have created the wheel of life used in our rules section earlier. He could also have invented penicillin, and for all I know he might even be laying claim to the motorcar as we speak. I have no idea who invented the S.M.A.R.T. formula, all that I do know is that it is the simplest way yet (besides perhaps using P.P.P. which means positive, personal and present tense) to define a goal specifically.

A poorly defined goal will only result in a poor picture being given to our unconscious mind. We must have absolute clarity so that we can see the result we are working towards. Although it has been around as long as Methuselah, the S.M.A.R.T. formula for goal setting is still the most effective way to define a goal precisely and with absolute clarity.

Believe You Can

We will elaborate a little by using the S.M.A.R.T.E.R. formula to define our MDP. Let me explain the S.M.A.R.T.E.R. formula for those who have no idea what I am talking about. The acronym means:

SPECIFIC
MEASURABLE
ACHIEVABLE
RELEVANT (Outboard trainers will tell you this is realistic)
TIME PHASED
EVALUATE
REWARD

A little about each might give you a better understanding of the process.

Specific means just what it says. Your MDP must be specific. I have lost count of the number of times I have heard people say that their goal is "to be happy" or "to be fitter," or even "to have more money." These are all very well but what does "to be happy" mean? If you can't answer that question with clarity how do you know that you are not already happy but you just don't realise it? How fit is "to be fitter?" For me it is to run a marathon in less than four hours nowadays. But to someone else it might just mean walking to the pub without having to sit down for a rest. And how much money is more money? To have a real chance of achieving your goals, and ultimately your MDP, you must be so specific it is almost as if you have the goal already.

Measurable means how will you know that you are getting there. How will you measure your progress? Losing weight is easy to measure, you just get on the scales every now and then and you can see whether what you are doing is working or not. But how do you measure happiness? Is not having a row with your partner for a month your way of measuring? Or would you have to be able to spend a certain amount of time with your family or friends, or doing whatever makes you happy, to know whether what you are doing is

Believe You Can

working or not? How will you know that what you are doing is working? It is not a difficult question to answer is it? ……….. Is it?

Achievable might be a strange thing to hear coming from someone who has just spent over a hundred pages telling you that you can achieve anything that you put your mind to. For an explanation of this one go back to the rules of goal setting and read the same stuff there about setting achievable goals.

Relevant is my way of saying *realistic,* which is what the outboard trainer or author will tell you it means. If they are correct by the way, then someone please tell me what the difference is between realistic and achievable. By my way of thinking your MDP has to be relevant to your other goals. In other words it has to be balanced with all of the other areas of your life. There is no point having an MDP to get your golf handicap down to single figures if one of your other goals is to double the turnover of your company. Likewise, nothing positive can come, as far as a balanced life is concerned, by having an MDP to at least double the time you spend with your family, and at the same time become an international athlete or speaker. Something has got to give in these cases.

Time phased again is an area that we covered in the rules of goal setting in an earlier chapter. Suffice to say that you are probably not going to lose forty-two pounds, or twenty (ish) kilograms, in weight, in less than a month. But if you take up to six months we are only talking ounces a day.

And now to the extra two that some of the others leave out.

Evaluate your MDP regularly. Check and see whether it is still as important to you as you once thought it was. Neither goals nor your MDP are meant to be cast in stone. Just because you have gone through the process of writing them down and committing to them, it does not mean that you cannot be a little flexible with them.

Believe You Can

Recently, Sara and I were forced to evaluate one of our lesser goals. We had a goal to fly to New York on Concord just for the thrill of it. However, through no fault of our own, we now have to evaluate that particular goal because Concord in no longer in service. We asked ourselves if travelling to New York on a 747 but travelling first class would be a relevant substitute. Our answer was a resounding no! It just wasn't Concord.

So because of the actions of someone else whose decisions we could not influence, we discarded our goal and carried on. This is not exactly life threatening I know. But what if your goal or MDP was a little more serious than flying on Concord? But for one reason or another, you decide that whatever it is, it is no longer relevant to your future happiness or perceived success? Evaluate your goal or MDP regularly. And if you think it necessary, change it into something that is relevant to your future happiness or perceived success. After all, it is your future we are talking about here not mine, or anyone else's for that matter.

Reward yourself for your efforts regularly. Some would say, and for the most part I agree with them, that achieving your goal or MDP is reward in itself. But what if your aims are extremely long-term? Or worse still, as happened to me when I completed my first Ironman triathlon in 1991, there is a massive anti-climax at the end of your journey. Rewarding yourself along the way and particularly at the end is a great way to remain focussed and motivated to see it through. Let's say for arguments sake that you have an MDP to increase your level of fitness and decrease your weight at the same time. Like many people, you might have decided to measure your success by the fact that you will be able to get into all of those clothes that you *used* to be able to fit into. Rewarding yourself like that is not the sort of reward that is likely to set you on fire. It is worth pointing out here that those clothes that you *used* to fit into actually represent a type of failure to your internal workings, simply because you *used* to be able to fit into them. The fact that you can't fit into them now might mean that you have in some way failed in the past. And these clothes are a symbol of that failure. Hmmmm, that's an interesting thought isn't it? You could give yourself an extra incentive to achieve your fitness and weight loss goals by promising to buy yourself, or even buying for yourself right now, an article of clothing that you have neither been able to fit into or afford in the past. Think about it. In order to achieve your MDP of becoming fitter (whatever that means to you) you will also have to achieve two intermediate goals. You will need to lose pounds in weight, and gain pounds in the monetary sense (nice play on words don't you think?) to firstly pay for your item of clothing and then to fit into it. So what have you achieved here by setting a MDP? You have achieved the MDP by becoming what you regard as fitter of course. But perhaps just as importantly, you have created a physical you that makes you happy and you have become more aware of your financial abilities by saving for something you previously thought you could not afford. How cool is that? Hey, it really works this stuff doesn't it?

On the next page is a handy diagram of the path we have just discussed that takes us from having dreams to defining our MDP. The category for "Toys and things" is a category for those things that you just want to play with. Not life changing things or objects that will ultimately determine your future success, just some of those things that you think that you deserve. Perhaps you could put some of your rewards in this category. You probably shouldn't take this category too seriously. For the record, one of the things in my toy category is to build myself a tree house. I never had a **real** tree house as a kid, none of the local farmers would let us in their fields long enough to establish the foundations. I have a vision that I am sat in my tree house reading a book and watching the world go by. By the way, I do have a tree that knows all of my secrets, doesn't everybody?

Defining your Major Definite Purpose:

Dreams and Ambitions

A Goal is a dream with a date attached

Goals

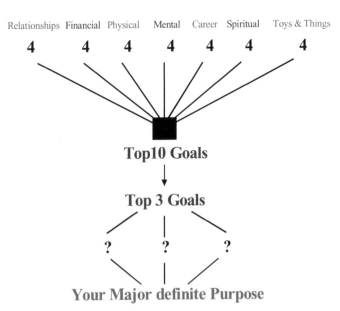

Your Major definite Purpose

"A non-negotiable goal that, when achieved, will have the
greatest positive impact on your future success"

There is one final important point that I should mention here. It is highly unlikely that you will stay constantly on course for achieving your goals and your *Major Definite Purpose* one hundred percent of the time. When an aeroplane takes off from wherever it is flying from to wherever it is going to, it is likely to be off course for at least some of the journey. You will be exactly the same. Certain things cleverly disguised as challenges will take you off course during the fantastic journey that you are setting off on. These challenges are just that, challenges. They are not permanent distractions. Just as the pilot of the aircraft will keep adjusting his course to stay on target for his or her destination you must do the same. Your direction change could be an illness, a cancellation or a disappointment in some other disguise. Whatever it is that the universe throws at you it is just a test of your courage and tenacity. Staying focussed on the goal or *Major Definite Purpose* rather than the time line will ensure that the pilot arrives safely, if a little late, at the intended destination. If you do the same you too will arrive safely at your destination, if a little late. And who knows, once you have achieved one thing that you thought was impossible perhaps nothing will ever seem impossible to you again. Perhaps whatever it is you want to become or to achieve, you too, like me and thousands of others, will *"Believe You Can."*

"Life is what happens while you are busy making other plans."
John Lennon

The ~~End~~ Beginning

So there you have it. You now have a collection of techniques and ideas, even some skills, which could help you to become the person that you have always dreamed of becoming. I sincerely hope that you have enjoyed reading the journey that is **Believe You Can** as much as I have enjoyed writing it.

For some of you this book will simply act as a reminder of all of those things that you used to do but have let slip. To others it might be "a good read but it's only common sense really isn't it?" And to others it might signal the start of a fantastic journey that I myself began in the early nineties when I read "How to Win Friends and Influence People" by Dale Carnegie and "Unlimited Power" by Anthony Robins. If you have as much fun and enlightenment as I have had, if you only meet half of the fantastic people that I have met, and if you achieve at least some of the peace of mind that I have achieved since reading those books, and the hundreds of others since, then your journey will be truly magnificent.

I thank you for honouring me by reading my book and I look forward to meeting as many of you as possible during our journey. I wish you health and happiness.

Live Life on Purpose.

"Most people overestimate what they can do in a year and underestimate what they can do in a lifetime."
Anon

"A journey of a thousand miles starts with one small step."
Confucius

A burning question

The burning question I had when I started this book was:

_____

_____

_____

I think that the answer to that question is:

_____

_____

_____

Now that I have the answer I *Believe I Can:*

_____

_____

_____

About the Author
Lardman to Ironman

Clive Gott left Tadcaster Grammar School in May of 1974 with little more than a report book that included such statements as "usually a nuisance, will probably amount to little" and "Gott needs to understand that he will get nowhere by talking all day!" Just eight years and twelve jobs later, and already in his second marriage, Clive joined North Yorkshire Fire Brigade on 13th February 1982. The day he joined he was six feet three inches tall and weighed around twelve stones seven pounds.

Four years later, on 5th January 1986, he was summoned to the station office by his commanding officer Mike Homer. The meeting was to discuss Clive's attitude to his work and the fact that he was now grossly overweight. So overweight that the doctor's scales showed that he did in fact weigh twenty stones and two pounds. The repercussions of that conversation are still evident today. Clive immediately enrolled in the local gymnasium and just three years later completed the 1989 London Marathon in an impressive three hours, six minutes and twenty-two seconds. His next challenge was to complete a triathlon. In October of 1989, Clive completed the Airbrough triathlon in Leeds. The race covered a five hundred-meter swim followed by a fifteen-mile cycle and finishing with a six-mile run. The race took him two hours, two minutes and two seconds.

Over the next few years he completed countless marathons and umpteen triathlons of varying distances. Clive eventually competed in his first of four Ironman distance races (two and a half-mile swim, one hundred and twelve-mile cycle and twenty-six mile run) in June 1991. His fastest time over the distance was nine hours and thirty-six minutes. The journey from Lardman to Ironman was complete.

In February of 1992, following his eighth operation on his knees, Clive left the Fire Brigade. His first job was as an attendant at a local swimming pool. There followed a few other jobs including one

Believe You Can

as a conductor selling tickets on Regional Railways Northeast. It was during this period that Clive started reading. The first book he read was "Unlimited Power" by Anthony Robins. This was quickly followed by "How to Win Friends and Influence People." The more he read the more Clive discovered that his story was not too far removed from those written about in the books he was reading. He was inspired. SO much so that he successfully applied for a sales position with the Dale Carnegie organisation in Leeds.

Fourteen months later Clive turned to his talent for inspirational and motivational speaking. He was recruited by a Sussex based training organisation. This was the apprenticeship he needed to give him the confidence to go it alone. On 10th June 1999, "Lighthouse Training Ltd" was registered with Companies House.

Like many new companies, Lighthouse Training Ltd had its share of ups and downs. However, within eighteen months, his client list was impressive. Testimonials to his ability to make a difference in people's lives could be obtained from the likes of Canon, Pioneer, Honda, Zurich, Channel 4 TV, BUPA … the list goes on. Now, in 2004, Clive is a published author. (The publishing rights to his first book "A Fathers Gift, Your Life in Your Words" have been donated to the charity "Dreams Come True.") He is also a regular contributor to trade magazines and newspapers. However, this book, "Believe You Can" will be his first official best seller.

Clive Gott is an outstanding speaker with a unique ability to keep an audience of one, to one thousand, amused and entertained whilst leaving them empowered to achieve their wildest dreams. His many overseas engagements have seen him presenting to audiences from Berlin to Bombay, from Dublin to Dubai. As for the future, well that is in the hands of only one person - Clive Gott himself. However, do not be at all surprised if, in the next few years, a book appears on the desks of every secondary school student in the United Kingdom. The book will be entitled "How to Become Unstoppable in Education and Life Beyond." The name of the author? I will leave that to you.

Believe You Can
Personal and Professional Development Programme

Clive's very effective Personal and Professional development programme "Believe You Can" has, and continues to be, delivered in some of the largest corporate and sporting organisations in the UK. Clive is now proud to include Europe and the United Arab Emirates as part of the global expansion in his goal to create a worldwide Mexican wave of enthusiasm, inspiration and positive thinking.

Following the programme, delegates have said that they now:

- Understand the benefits of controlling their attitude
- Understand how to control their attitude
- Understand how low self-esteem affects their performance
- Have developed higher self-esteem
- Are able to enhance and develop the self-esteem of others
- Have developed an attitude of personal responsibility
- Understand the basic skills involved in, and the importance of, effective communication
- Learned the difference between limiting and empowering self-beliefs
- Understand why, and how, successful people set goals
- Learned how to set and achieve personal and professional goals that are suitable for them
- Have a series of goals and an action plan for their achievement

For more information about our corporate in-house or our public **Believe You Can** programmes, go to *www.clivegott.com*

Information

Other publications by Clive Gott:

Believe and Achieve audio programme

Inspiration on Tap audio programme

Live Life on Purpose audio and workbook

27 Proven Ways to Grow Your Business audio and booklet

Believe You Can personal development programme

Clive Gott is highly skilled in delivering presentations, from keynote speeches to five-day development programmes.

To find out more about his very effective "Believe You Can" development programme or other keynote speeches and workshops, go to:

www.clivegott.com

Or contact Clive at:

**Clive Gott
15 Toll Bar Way
Tadcaster
North Yorkshire
LS24 8JT
England**

**Tel: + 44 (0) 1937 832509
Email: clive@clivegott.com**